FOLLOWING THE FULHAM
AROUND THE GROUNDS

Pippa

with love from

Peter

Please see page 140

FOLLOWING THE FULHAM AROUND THE GROUNDS

PETER THOMSON

ASHWATER
PRESS

First published in October 2003

Copyright © Peter Thomson 2003

The right of Peter Thomson to be identified as the author
of all original material in this book has been asserted by him
in accordance with the Copyright, Designs and Patent Act 1988

Designed and published for Peter Thomson by
Ashwater Press
68 Tranmere Road, Whitton, Twickenham, Middlesex, TW2 7JB

Printed and bound by Butler & Tanner, Frome

ISBN 0 9538840 7 4

SENTIMENTAL JOURNEY

Gonna take a sentimental journey
Round the grounds we want to be.
Gonna take a sentimental journey,
Sincil Bank and Highbury.

Gonna make a sentimental journey
Round the grounds both far and near.
Gonna make a sentimental journey,
Blackpool Tower and Brighton Pier.

Ready for a sentimental journey
Round the grounds both near and far.
Ready for a sentimental journey,
Stamford Bridge and Ballygar.

Gonna take a sentimental journey
Twerton, Ashford, Vetch and Shay.
Gonna take a sentimental journey,
Meadow Lane and Meadow Gay.

Got to take a sentimental journey
To those teams beside the sea.
Got to take a sentimental journey,
Southend, Scarborough, Split, Torquay.

Got to make a sentimental journey
All aboard that special train.
Just MUST make one final journey—
Craven Cottage, home again.

August 2003.

With acknowledgements/apologies to B Green, L Brown, B Horner.

CONTENTS

INTRODUCTION

Following the Fulham celebrated 50 seasons at Craven Cottage. The 50th season being that truly extraordinary explosion of talent and technique which enabled Tigana's team to win the first 11 matches and then coast to the title with 101 points. Promotion to the Premiership posed problems which were touched upon in the final chapters but a publication date of November 2001 excluded serious consideration of the new stadium.

Come the second edition in January 2002 there was talk of ground sharing but little detail was available. By May 2002 we knew we were off to Loftus Road, we had escaped relegation and we had qualified for the Intertoto challenge. By late August 2002 we were unbeaten after eight matches in five countries and it seemed appropriate to celebrate the cup with an extra chapter, hence the booklet *Following the Fulham Into Europe*.

Subsequent matches against Split, Zagreb and Berlin demanded recognition—recognition which by December 2002 had to be entitled "Out of Europe". Hardly an inspiring title and hardly a publisher's dream but the essays were prepared and the photos entrusted to Ken Coton.

"Out of Europe" sounded sad but "Out of the Cottage" sounded sinister. Rumour, counter rumour, speculation and controversy about Craven Cottage resulted in a winter of discontent, and all made worse by uncertainty over Tigana's contract.

Anxiety and petulance may cloud some of these pages but David Lloyd liked the essay on York and the finished article is now available at TOOFIF corner, South Africa Road, on match days. By the 'finished article' I mean *Following the Fulham Around the Grounds*. Craven Cottage—the finished article? As in August 1986 so too in August 2003—who knows?

Peter Thomson, Mortlake, August 2003

ACKNOWLEDGEMENTS

Every picture tells a story. Here are some more pictures and lots more stories. Most of the football photos were taken by Ken Coton and the stories are all the better for his visual aids. All the pictures have been processed by him at Ashwater Press. As editor, Ken has improved the text but the faults/follies/ fantasies are mine. Without Ken, *Around The Grounds* would have been less easy on the eye and much less fun to write.

My thanks again to Dennis Turner and Alex White for their excellent reference books on our club, most particularly *Fulham Facts and Figures*. The chairman, directors and officers of FFC have provided me with 52 years worth of material, match magazines and a second home. I gratefully acknowledge the club in the production of this book. My thanks also to David Lloyd and *TOOFIF* for help and inspiration.

The book *Football Fanatic* and its author have helped me in my travels around the grounds. Ken Ferris visited 93 different grounds in a single season and published his tour guide. His account is as informative as John Ley's *Kick Off* and rather more readable.

"*Back home…*" Within the family there are those for whom the day out is almost as important as the match itself. The journey, the setting, the atmosphere, the company, the conversation, the creature comforts, all add to or detract from following the Fulham. Piers and I enjoy the noise at Loftus Road, but the location, the restricted view and the lack of leg room alienated many Fulham fans. My wife, Sheila, enjoyed recent visits to Bologna, Split, Zagreb and Stamford Bridge but she cut back on 'home' fixtures, so our second season ticket has been taken up by Jeremy Fordham. I miss Sheila but value Jeremy's judicious comments. Sheila and Jeremy have helped with proof reading. My thanks to them both.

Come May 2004 and the ordering of season tickets, let it be Craven Cottage; that should bring Sheila back to her seat by the riverside, back home… "Home, sweet home."

PFT

ILLUSTRATIONS

Most of the photographs are by the author or Ken Coton. In addition, grateful thanks are due to the following for permission to use their pictures: Mrs M Collier—page 56; Les Coverdale—22 and 53; Peter Gibson—134; Grimsby FC—40; Steven Hatch—44; Ipswich FC—51; Rettie family—73 and 74; Mrs H Sommer—81; TOOFIF—97; Alan Williams—129.

GROUND RULES

For the purposes of this volume a ground is not a ground unless Fulham have been there. Thus Wembley is a ground because we were there in '75 but Cardiff means Ninian Park not the Millennium Stadium. Fulham know the former well; they are still preparing for the latter. Much as I enjoyed watching the Pilgrims playing the Seagulls at Boston, that engaging Fenland stadium can't be included because I have not followed the Fulham there.

Nomenclature—tricky word for a tricky subject. Let us start with our own beloved club. Last season we kicked off in July at Craven Cottage, so that was our ground. Come August 17th we were beating Bolton in the Premiership at Loftus Road so has that become our ground? As for the future we will be playing at…? Thus FFC has to be discussed under F for Fulham.

Unfortunately going around the grounds can't be done in the traditional manner: club 92. Attractive as Cheltenham and Kidderminster might be, they are not yet following the Fulham grounds and are thus excluded. Doncaster and Hereford may not be of the elite 92 but they have felled the followers of the Fulham and are therefore grounds.

I have gone for the alphabetical approach: following the Fulham from humble non-league Ashford to mighty World Cup grounds such as Berlin and Bologna. Hooray, hooray for the Intertoto adventure—it brought us many new grounds and gained us access to Europe. It even enabled this alphabetical journey to terminate in the Maksimir Stadium at Zagreb. What a destination and what a result! Dinamo Zagreb 0 Ulham 3.

From Arsenale to Zagreb via Venice. My wife, Sheila, wearing her Fulham hat.

Hold the Front Page

Newsflash, 3rd September 2003: "Fulham to return to Craven Cottage."
Rapture.
Statement, 3rd September 2003: "Chairman delighted…to take us home, albeit temporarily."
Modified rapture.
Fulhamish, of course, to be uncertain. Uncertain whether to rejoice at the word 'home' or fret about 'albeit temporarily'. Fulhamish uncertainty as to whether our glass is half empty or half full.

Followers of the Fulham born in, or before, 1939 have mixed emotions each 3rd September. Mindful of past history and statements such as "peace in our time" it seems prudent to reserve the very best champagne for August 2004—when we are indeed 'Back at the Cottage'.

On hearing the news... Author clutching at straws and orange juice; grandson Olivier chewing on something stronger; wife Sheila counting down to August 2004 and that champagne celebration.

EDITOR'S NOTE:

This book was put together before the announcement of the club's return to Craven Cottage, hence the many references to doubts about the club's future location. Bearing in mind the nature of the announcement, readers are invited either to indulge the author's pre-September thoughts or still consider such doubts valid.

Arsenal

The Arsenal: the aristocrats of London, never out of the top flight, League and Cup double in 1971 and 2002. The Arsenal have marble halls while we have (had) a cottage. The Arsenal have won everything while we have the Intertoto cup/cuplet. In 90 years we have beaten them five times at the Cottage but we have never won at Highbury. We may never beat them there because they are planning bigger and better than those mighty marbled halls.

On January 18th 1964 my birthday present from Johnny Haynes was the equaliser in the Arsenal fixture and we have not managed anything as distinguished at Highbury since then. I set out for N5 on 23rd February 2002 determined to be there after an absence of 33 years but without much hope of a point. At the Cottage in September we had been outclassed and beaten 3–1. At Highbury we froze off the pitch as snow fell on the visitors' end. We froze on the pitch as the Gunners shot us to pieces. A good header from Marlet made it 1–1 for a minute or two but Arsenal soon scored again. Come half-time I gulped at the Bovril with Nick and Charles Wood. We agreed that we would be lucky to get out 1–5. Lucky we were when Mr Wenger removed Thierry Henry early thus allowing us to escape 4–1 down.

Down and out, to be honest—because the Arsenal were far too good for us in every department. Not so in 2002 when Marlet scored again (for them)

We never do well at Arsenal. Jim Langley shoots in February 1965, but we lose 2–0.

in a much more even contest. The referee later agreed that he ought to have awarded us a penalty or two. Too late, Mr Winter, too late; Arsenal had already made off with all three points. At Highbury we were less intimidated this season: Sean Davis stood up to Vieira while Maik Taylor made several great saves. Steed Malbranque with his fifth goal in a week equalised the early header from Pires and it seemed that we might hang on for a point. Not so because deep into injury time Pires scored again. Anguish, of course, but not despair because we had improved and competed with the champions. Competed with but could not emulate, for the Arsenal of today is not the erratic Arsenal of those *Fever Pitch* years. Now, under Wenger, they have achieved that total football which enables them to dominate and illuminate the Premiership year upon year. Fulham dominated the first division with classy, stylish football for one season. Arsenal perform with class and style at a higher level season after season. Admirable Arsenal, we salute you.

Ashford Town

From the sublime to the ridiculous, from mighty Highbury to humble Homelands, from the heights of the Champions League to the depths of Doc Martenland, from the best playing surface in London to the worst pitch in Kent—indeed, according to Micky Adams, "the worst pitch I have ever encountered". From the Arsenal to Ashford Town.

If we were unlucky to lose in the 90th minute at Highbury in February 2003 we were very fortunate not to be three goals down at the Homelands/ Wetlands on 12th November 1994. To lose to the champions at Highbury is one thing but to be booted out of the FA Cup by non-leaguers is another. We had lost to Hayes in 1991 and to Yeovil in 1993; was it to be the same again in 1994?

This was as strange a contest as any I have witnessed in 52 seasons of following the Fulham. The first hint of the unconventional came from our man Magee with whom I took tea on the Friday. Wellington boots were advised and Wellington boots were essential. Many Fulham fans were waterlogged in the Ashford car park and the pitch contained several lakes long before Mr D'Urso authorised play. Heavy rain continued throughout the match until the entire surface was under water. *Match of the Day* cameras and BBC cheque books must have influenced the clubs in the agreement to play and in the end there was a game. What a game it was and yet—what game was it?

Emma Hawkey printed my account of events in the Fulham programme but my camera failed me. I wish that I could offer photographs of fans perched on walls after the duckboards floated away. Mike Jones in his montage featured Robert Haworth with face covered in mud. It took superhuman vision to see any action as the darkness fell and the floodlights flickered but Mr D'Urso saw a trip, a trip here and a hand-ball there enabling Micky Adams to right some wrongs from the penalty spot/puddle. Final score: Ashford Town 2 Fulham 2.

After the great escape on the pitch, we prepared for the great escape off the pitch. Our coach driver had sensibly remained at the main road so we squelched away to rejoin him and attempted to dry out with some topical songs: "Singing in the Rain", "Man the Lifeboats" and "Micky Adams walks on Water". David Roodyn and the Chef spotted the signposts to the channel tunnel and sang us: "Into Europe, Into Europe". Sing up and dream on, but come the 7th of August 2002 there I was back at Ashford for the Eurostar to Paris/Dijon/Sochaux and the semi-final of the Intertoto Cup. Thus via Sochaux and Bologna to Split, Zagreb and Berlin: "Into Europe…"

Into Europe via Ashford Town.

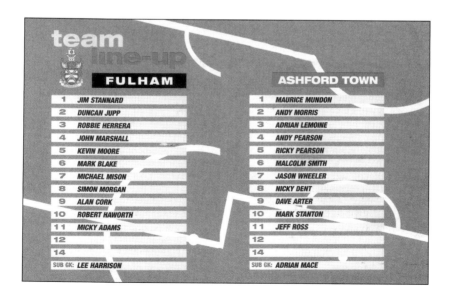

	team line-up FULHAM		ASHFORD TOWN
1	JIM STANNARD	1	MAURICE MUNDON
2	DUNCAN JUPP	2	ANDY MORRIS
3	ROBBIE HERRERA	3	ADRIAN LEMOINE
4	JOHN MARSHALL	4	ANDY PEARSON
5	KEVIN MOORE	5	RICKY PEARSON
6	MARK BLAKE	6	MALCOLM SMITH
7	MICHAEL MISON	7	JASON WHEELER
8	SIMON MORGAN	8	NICKY DENT
9	ALAN CORK	9	DAVE ARTER
10	ROBERT HAWORTH	10	MARK STANTON
11	MICKY ADAMS	11	JEFF ROSS
12		12	
14		14	
SUB GK:	LEE HARRISON	SUB GK:	ADRIAN MACE

"Let's Go Round the Grounds"

Over to our own correspondent. "Let's go round the grounds" is all part of the ritual on BBC and LBC. At LBC our own correspondent in the 1980s and 1990s was Jonathan Sim. Jonathan has followed the Fulham for many years and when matters were going from bad (1986) to worse (1994–1996) it would be: "Over to the Undertaker for news of Fulham."

Jonathan did his best for FFC but they did not do much for him or for us. In September 1993 it was "Over to the Undertaker for news of another Burnley goal" and later that same month it was "Over to the Undertaker who has news of another defeat for Fulham" (away to Huddersfield).

Over to the Undertaker for our funeral at the Vetch in May 1994 and over to the Undertaker at the Bescot Stadium in September 1994 for Walsall 5 Fulham 1. Jonathan reported on life in the lower leagues with accuracy and melancholy. Every inch the Undertaker, his sombre tones were not made for 1997 or 1999 or 2001. Those promotion years took Jonathan out of the press box and back to the terraces. He teamed up with Patrick Mascall and contributed to match magazines and *Fultime*.

Come the crisis of April 2003 and who had returned to the microphone for Fulham 0 Blackburn 4? Inevitably/indubitably/incomparably—the Undertaker with the lugubrious and laconic greeting: "Team in disarray; club in disarray."

Undertaker to the left, lawyer to the right. Fulham forum at the Valley, 11th May 2003.

Berlin

An exciting prospect for all and a new ground for most of us. Derek the Frame and I booked good and early for this UEFA Cup fixture with Hertha Berlin, 25th November 2002. We enjoyed an easy and inexpensive flight with a fast and comfortable bus ride from the airport to the city centre. Our hotel was near the zoo, placed between a distinguished modern church and a bizarre museum of erotica.

Up early on match day to visit the Reichstag before meeting followers of the Fulham at the Brandenburg Gate. Group photographs and coffee at Michael Jackson's Hotel Adlon. Highly efficient rail links to the Olympic Stadium (unlike our own late beloved Wembley) and we were out there by 4pm to see this vast ground by daylight.

For followers of the Fulham born before September 1939 this Olympic stadium comes with powerful and painful images. The whole area is derelict but millions of Euro are about to be devoted to reconstruction in ample time for the next World Cup.

At dusk on 26th November 2002 the Berlin stadium was deserted/depressing/spooky. At the Cottage the spirits of J block are benign but in Berlin malign spectres haunt the woods around the ground. Perhaps I was imagining these shades of Nazism but other much younger followers of the Fulham were also uneasy in the ruined areas of the Olympic stadium.

Once inside matters went from the numinous to the luminous with floodlights picking out the 14,447 spectators scattered around a 96,000 seater/ruin. Next to the Fulham enclosure were cranes, bulldozers and mountains of sand. Bologna, Split and Zagreb had noise, fireworks and atmosphere but Berlin was disappointing—dismal

Jimmy and friend (large friend) at the Brandenburg Gate. Where were they in '89 when the wall came down? Following the Fulham at Port Vale.

surroundings and a dismal first half. Hertha Berlin offered little and Fulham offered less. We were caught cold by a well worked free kick and were one goal down at the interval. The introduction of Boa Morte transformed the second half as he set up three good chances in ten minutes. We hit the bar, the net, and their keeper. Marlet's goal seemed to be enough until a spectacular slice from Sava was far beyond van der Sar and gifted the evening to Hertha Berlin. We defended well in the last few minutes and at the whistle the Fulham fans were talking up the value of the away goal against a dour team with limited attacking options.

The return to the city centre was swift and troublefree; the evening meal and match analysis proved enjoyable until an arrogant Berliner accused us of short changing the waiter. Professor Roodyn and I had sufficient German to force a retraction. Slowly and patiently we recounted the Euro in his hand before departing with the Parthian shot: "Genug ist genug."

Enough perhaps to defend the integrity of Fulham's followers but not enough to keep intact that proud record "undefeated in Europe since 1973".

Grounds for Divorce

Following the Fulham around the grounds and over land and sea—yes, the courts have recognised this as 'unreasonable behaviour'. Some fans have lost a wife or two between Wembley in 1975 and the Premiership in 2001. My wife has been more than understanding and sensibly selective. Seaside fixtures, certainly—thus Bournemouth and Brighton, Exeter and Grimsby, Portsmouth and Torquay, Scarborough and Split are definitely Mr AND Mrs Thomson. University and cathedral fixtures—probably together, with frequent visits to Oxford and Cambridge and this summer Bologna as a glorious addition to the university scene. Sadly no Mrs Thomson at York for last season's FA Cup nor at Berlin for this season's UEFA fixture.

What of Barnsley and Bradford, Rotherham and Rochdale, Walsall and West Brom? Not for my wife, and how right she has almost always been. More pain than gain among those dark satanic mills.

Bologna

August the 13th, 2002. To the stadium Renato Dall'Ara to watch Fulham play Bologna, a vast arena which hosts international fixtures and was a World Cup ground back in June 1990. A warm evening and a noisy crowd of 23,420 Italians making good humoured mock of the 200 followers of the Fulham tucked away in one corner of the stadium. After Egaleo and Sochaux we were used to police and soldiers but the dog handlers of Bologna were particularly hard on their hounds.

The match was terrific and was contested at a faster pace than any of the earlier Intertoto fixtures. Bologna had the full complement of duckers and divers; dive they did and eventually secured a penalty converted by the veteran international Signori. Fulham fans were becoming anxious as the referee seemed to be losing control but Jean Tigana steadied our nerves by sending on Inamoto. George Best scored in the first minute of his Fulham career but he just took a pass, a touch and a shot. Inamoto made a tackle, beat two defenders and curled a left-footed shot beyond Bologna's international keeper Pagliuca. 1–1 and a sensational start for Inamoto.

Just as we sensed victory the divers took over and Bologna were awarded a second penalty which Signori thrashed past van der Sar. Indignation in the Fulham ranks but we were still full of running and Louis Saha set up Legwinski for a well directed shot. 2–2 and no less than we deserved.

"Some of their players can cheat and provoke and try to disturb my team." Jean Tigana was not happy with such Bolognese antics but once the match was over the Italian crowd were more than generous. Our police coaches were surrounded by the good folk of Bologna who waved and cheered our return to the city centre where we were immediately welcomed to the street party (a festival of lights and hot air balloons.)

Come midnight in the cathedral square Sheila and I retired to our hotel but Alex the Traveller was warming to his work as musical adviser to the town band. Followers of the Fulham knew the words to *Blue Moon* and boosted the local choir for an hour or three. An enjoyable end to an enjoyable chapter in Fulham's Eurostory.

Bologna in August was bliss, far better than Rome and Florence. As a culture vulture in the 50s (long before Intertoto had been invented) I used to work my way around the museums and galleries of Italy. Florence and Rome were overcrowded then and are impossible now but Bologna… Bologna is a mediaeval masterpiece and deserted in August. Sheila was initially a little disappointed that certain shops were closed for the month but she soon warmed to the art and architecture. In addition she was mightily impressed by the football ground. Where in England can you find an Olympic swimming pool as part of the stadium? Doncaster Dome? Yes but Doncaster Dome is not part of the football ground and the Doncaster pool is indoors. Where in the world do you spend the morning swimming and lazing by the pool while your husband bumbles about on the diving board photographing the football ground? Bologna certainly; Split possibly but the outdoor pool is tiny and you might get shot when you produce your camera.

Dante may not know the words to *Blue Moon* but, like Inamoto, he got it right on the night of 13th August 2002: Puro e disposto a salire alle stelle— Bologna, stairway to the stars.

Bologna—a pool beside the ground. Almost as good as a river beside your ground.

Brighton

*B*righton Rock/Oh, What a Lovely War/Tommy and the Pinball Wizard—
film upon film, location upon location plus all that history from the
Prince Regent and Mrs Fitzherbert to the IRA bombers and Mrs Thatcher.
Brighton and Hove have often been more than the Albion.

Almost always the day by the sea has been better than the actual football.
Delighted as we were with the Pike and Hails goals in 1992 the match was
made by the Traveller and Captain Beakie who had walked all the way from
Craven Cottage in aid of Fulham 2000. The lengthy cup tie of 1995 was
finally rescued by the penalty shoot-out and Tony Lange's dramatic
intervention but the evening for me was dominated by an incident off the
ball and off the pitch. It was bitterly cold and far too rough for walking the
sea front. I sought sanctuary in the Brighton Museum where there is a vast
old fashioned stove in the main gallery. Leaning on this stove was an ancient
and fragrant tramp while in the far corner Harold Pinter and Lady Antonia
Fraser examined the Turners. Daniel Pinter and Orlando Fraser had been
pupils of mine hence conversations in the tea room before I set out for the
Goldstone. I knew of Pinter's passion for cricket but he talked me through

Old Fulham at old pier at old Goldstone.

his prowess as a footballer and a track athlete. "At school I was known as
Pinter the Sprinter." How we could have used his pace in the nasty 90s.

Barry Lloyd and Alan Mullery might not have matched Pinter the Sprinter
for pace but they both captained Fulham in the 70s. Lloyd leading Fulham to

promotion in 1971 and Mullery taking us all the way to Wembley in 1975. They worked together at the Goldstone from 1986 and Lloyd took over as manager of Brighton after Mullery.

In August 1995 we were three goals up from the first leg at the Cottage when we visited the Goldstone for a League Cup fixture. Sheila and I put the bikes on the train and enjoyed a pleasant afternoon on the beach at Hove. We were early to our seats which had been donated by the club. We found ourselves next to Barry Lloyd who was more than happy to talk about the

A great strike from Barry Lloyd— at Hull in 1975.

good old days under Alec Stock. Barry's sprinting days were done/undone come '95—I have never known any athlete get through so many cigarettes in 90 minutes. Fulham added goals through Conroy and Brazil; thus an aggregate 5–0 win completed a happy day beside the seaside, beside the sea.

Wembley in May 1983: "Smith must score…" Smith must score and Brighton must beat Man Utd in the final of the FA Cup. Smith didn't score and Brighton lost the replay. Brighton fell into the third division and lost the Goldstone. "Busby must score…" Busby didn't score and Fulham lost at Wembley. Fulham fell into the third division and Fulham lost the Cottage. Not only did Brighton recruit a goodly number of the Micky Adams team, Brighton recruited a goodly number of Fulham hearts…a favourite away day to Sussex. "Oh Sussex, Sussex by the sea…"

Cambridge

Back in 1961 when Spurs did the double there was an exhibition match in Cambridge followed by a reception for the players at Trinity College. The Master of Trinity, Lord Adrian, was an Olympic athlete and a Nobel Prize scientist but he had little time for football and asked me to host the reception. Spurs players kept themselves to themselves in one corner but the Cambridge team were a very friendly lot remaining on long after the Spurs coach returned to London.

In 1961 Cambridge United were in the Southern League and did not enter the fourth division until 1970. I never visited the Abbey Stadium as an undergraduate and never thought that Fulham would actually play Cambridge United. Certainly the very idea of Fulham being in the fourth/third division was preposterous and yet between 1978 and 1997 not only were we playing Cambridge we were losing to them—regularly.

Cambridge thrashed us 4–0 in December 1979 and 3–0 in January 1994. Even when we had a good side the Abbey Stadium would bring out the very worst in us. Super Mac's team of '82 almost, almost, made it back to the top flight but we stumbled at Cambridge just when we needed points to keep ahead of Leicester. In 1983 we escaped from a freezing Abbey Stadium with a precious point thanks to Kevin Lock. (For once Lock missed with his penalty kick but he followed up to put away the rebound.) In 1990–91 we lost three times to Cambridge—in the Cup and both league matches. In 1993-94 home and away league defeats contributed to our relegation slide.

Refuge, sanctuary and creature comforts were sought at Trinity College whenever Sheila and I followed the Fulham to the Abbey Stadium. Lord Adrian and his successors were more than generous. The worse the football the better the B&B. Three-nil down in the wind and rain meant an immediate upgrade to the Great Court guest room and the royal bed. That bed was comfortable but it was the vast deep bath which saved us from the ice of 1983 and the rains of 1994 and 1996.

Would we ever win a league match at Cambridge? Eventually, eventually we did. The date? It was the third of May 1997. Simon Morgan's brother Jon chose Fulham rather than Villa that day, Muriel was over from Paris, Ronny the Florist had the Carling prize limo...it was sunshine and smiles with 4,500 followers of the Fulham outsinging and outdancing the 2,700 home supporters.

The worse the football, the better the B&B. Author writes his match report before retiring into Trinity College's royal (Victoria and Albert) bed.

Lunch by the river, punts decked out in black and white, 3pm game on, and a Haynes of a through ball from Conroy to Freeman who rounded the keeper. Fulham 1 Cambridge 0. Bogey ground became boogie ground, jinx ground became jive ground. For many of our younger supporters it was their very first promotion party, for senior citizens it was our first major celebration in 16 years. Young and old had fun in the sun.

Degree day in Cambridge is always a colourful occasion. My degree day June 1961 was a first-class affair after four years of academic endeavour but 3 May 1997 was better, better, much better: the whole Fulham family graduating with honours after 16 years hard labour—a carnival in Cambridge, a fiesta for FFC.

Carnival teams from the Cambridge programme.

CAMBRIDGE UNITED	FULHAM
1 Scott BARRETT	1 Mark WALTON
2 Ian ASHBEE	2 Matt LAWRENCE
3 Paul WILSON	3 Paul WATSON
4 David PREECE	4 Nick CUSACK
5 Jody CRADDOCK	5 Danny CULLIP
6 Paul RAYNOR	6 Mark BLAKE
7 Paul WANLESS	7 Darren FREEMAN
8 Micah HYDE	8 Glenn COCKERILL
9 John TAYLOR	9 Mike CONROY
10 Jamie BARNWELL	10 Simon MORGAN
11 Marc JOSEPH	11 Richard CARPENTER
12 Michael KYD	12
13 Trevor BENJAMIN	13
14 Adie HAYES	14

On your Bike

Cycling to the Cottage is/was a joy, particularly in early autumn and late spring. In all those years (1951–2002) only one bike was nicked and that was after an evening game away at Chester where goals from Tempest and Coney eased the walk back to Barnes at 3am.

My wife was always happy to cycle to Craven Cottage but she has little enthusiasm for bike rides to Loftus Road. If we go there together it is the 283 bus from Barnes Pond. Left to my own devices, I still favour two wheels following the river to Hammersmith Bridge and then via the back streets to Melina Road where The Crown and Sceptre offers a distinguished menu and Adnam's ales—the double Delia for ex Hammersmith Enders.

Community service—Simon Morgan directing traffic.

Griffin Park and Stamford Bridge are well within cycling distance but for the rest of London I favour the Underground/metro/tube. The bike comes into its own again in the provinces. Have you noticed how far the ground is from Reading station? Elm Park was too far and the Madejski is even further. Stick the bike in the guards van and the long slog from station to ground becomes tolerable, enjoyable even, after winning goals from Skinner in '89 and Morgs in '99.

Best of all by bike is the free-wheeling from Brighton station down to the seafront and then a 15-minute pedal and a 15-minute paddle at the Hove end of town before climbing up to the Goldstone. Indeed consolation in a bad season was the 3–2 victory at Brighton after 13 games without a win. Many's the time I have cycled past Fulham fans on the seafront at Brighton. They shout out the traditional greeting: "London to Brighton bike ride was last week, Pete!"

Cyclist, season ticket holder and proof reader—thank you, Jeremy.

The Fulham ranks include a dedicated road racer in Mike Anderson but even he would salute the magnificent Rob Allen who biked all the way to Motherwell in November '75.

Following the Fulham around the grounds by bike and train—Bournemouth, Blackpool, Brighton, Cambridge, Chester, Chesterfield, Colchester, Crystal Palace, Exeter, Hereford, Ipswich, Lincoln, Shrewsbury, Swansea, Torquay, Wrexham and York. More Raleigh/Dunlop nationwide than Barclaycard Premiership, but healthy, very, very healthy.

Chelsea

Promotion to the Premiership in 2001 meant back to the Bridge and back in business with the Blues. For followers of the Fulham the Chelsea fixture is the one we have been longing for since November 1985 when we lost the League Cup replay. For us Fulham v Chelsea is THE derby match and week in week out for 16 years there were songs about blue flags and just where they should be placed.

Not so for Chelsea—they look down on us as just another little club. Fulham fell off football's inner circle in the 1980s and took a branch line off to Leyton Orient and Barnet but Chelsea won the FA Cup twice and added European honours in 1998. Chairman Bates was busy building bigger and better or bigger and bolder. International managers Ruud and ruder, Vialli and Ranieri plus international players by the dozen. For New Chelsea we were just minor league minnows. The long awaited match at Craven Cottage in September 2001 turned out to be a tame 1–1 draw curiously lacking in buzz and nothing like the pulsating and passionate encounters of my youth. Nothing like the shuddering, juddering contests of my son's youth. The best birthday party I ever hosted for Ian was Fulham 2 Chelsea 0 in September

FULHAM v CHELSEA

Howe Conway

2 — 0

Football League Division Two
Saturday 27 September 1975   Kick-off 3.00 pm
Official Matchday Magazine 15p

1975. Blood and thunder at the Cottage followed by a fish and chip tea for ten. Ian and his friends enjoyed it and I loved it, really, really loved it.

Chelsea back at the Cottage after 15 years was an anti-climax—but our first FA Cup semi-final for 26 years and against Chelsea, now that was something. Yes, it was bathos, pathos and worse; wrong day (Sunday) wrong time (7pm). A nothing goal in a nothing game sent Chelsea through to Cardiff. We were back to the relegation dog fight. Irony of ironies, it took a Chelsea reject (Bjarne Goldbaek) to lift us at Elland Road and save us by burying Bolton.

In September 2002 the home game was scoreless and nowhere near as noisy as Spurs, Man Utd, Liverpool, Villa. Truth to tell the badinage was better with the Bologna, Split, Zagreb, Berlin supporters. Shed-enders are not what they used to be. After we beat them 3–1 on Good Friday 1977 they smashed every shop window in the Fulham Palace Road, and Easter Monday saw them demolishing a substantial section of the main stand at Charlton. "Arson, blue lace and a boot in yer face…"

In October 1979 Fulham were in trouble at the wrong end of the second division while Chelsea were celebrating six wins out of six. At Stamford Bridge, against all the odds, we won and won with ease 2–0. I was at the Cottage on the Monday morning to collect tickets from Sandra and saw Bobby Campbell unlocking his car. "Congratulations and thank you," said I. Campbell retorted with a less than gracious diatribe against followers of the Fulham who only cared about the Chelsea result. Astounded I protested my devotion from Haynes even unto the present day, with which he calmed down and offered me a lift to Hammersmith Bridge. I declined pointing to my bicycle and we went our separate ways. Campbell, of course, to join the coaching staff at Chelsea where his manner may have been appreciated on the training ground and in the Shed. Chopper Harris and Micky Droy had thicker skins than John Mitchell who frequently suffered at the hands/tongue of Mr Campbell.

Chopper Harris, Micky Droy, Joey Jones on the pitch winding up the mob from the Shed—only Millwall could rival Old Chelsea. Between 1986 and 2001 there have been changes at the Bridge, changes physical and changes metaphysical. The National Front and the Chelsea Headhunters have gone.

Dennis Wise was probably the last of the old guard. The present Chelsea squad blends every colour, class and creed into a highly talented team playing attractive and effective football. Zola is a truly distinguished ambassador for Chelsea—witness the standing ovation accorded to him at Craven Cottage. Impossible to remember any such tributes to Butch Wilkins, Chopper Harris, Blunstone, Webb, McCreadie, Droy or Jones in their visits to Fulham during the 70s and 80s.

Our return to the Bridge in March 2002 was more like it with end to end football, loads of noise and loads of goals. At 2–2 Fulham had their purple patch and the Chelsea crowd sensed trouble until super sub Forsell poached the late, late winner. We departed disappointed, but at least we had been to a real match, a proper battle of Stamford Bridge.

April 2003 and back to the Bridge with Chelsea looking for a place in the Champions' League and Fulham fighting for survival. Chelsea fans had spent the week making mock and counting the points. Sheila and I

Chelsea pensioner. Peter Bonetti helps out at Motspur Park.

and I feared the worst but took our seats in good time and were rewarded with a smile, a wave and a friendly word from Ivor. Immediately we recalled his goal from October 1979 and took heart. Coleman's tactics frustrated Chelsea for most of the first half and when they did score it involved a dive from Le Saux, a stumble by Taylor, a hand from Terry, all adding up (apparently) to Goma o.g.

Come the second half Chelsea became impatient. Taylor saved us again and again as the Shed grumbled at Hasselbaink. Boa Morte turned Desailly inside out, twice, before curling a shot into the far corner of the net. It looked good at the time and (five replays later) it looked even better on TV. John Collins almost won the match in injury time but most of us were happy with a point and a pint.

Weeks later I am still chuckling at two Fulhamish quips in response to the remorseless chanting of Chelsea fans: "Lampard for England, Lampard for England!" First came Taylor's astonishing double save then up jumped Freddie Fulham: "Lampard for Finland? Lampard for Finland?" Freddie Fulham got no ground, but still got repartee.

Chelsea demolished their Archibald Leitch stand to make way for the new stadium. We poured Fulham 2000's money into our Stevenage Road Stand. Preservation and restoration, heritage and history, thus the Archibald Leitch contribution to Craven Cottage is a handsome listed facade. A facade protected but to what purpose? We want a football ground not a museum. We want our home, sweet home, not a heritage centre.

Ken Bates transformed and saved Chelsea. Then he offered to transform and 'save' Fulham. The unthinkable and unmentionable had been thought and mentioned. Jimmy Hill our chairman from 1987 to 1997 (our anti-merger chairman) contacted both Bates and Al Fayed and campaigned for a groundshare at the Bridge. However, new Wealthski at Chelski has moved more than goalposts. Overnight Ken Bates and Jimmy Hill are yesterday's men. The summer of 2003 belonged to the young Russian. So far (end of August) he has not bought any of our players. Good. He flew over our ground and did not like the look of it. Phew! What a relief. Let Chelsea concentrate on chasing the Arsenal and Man United. Then perhaps, as on Good Friday 1977 and on 27th October 1979, pride might come before their fall.

Derby

Difficult to write objectively about Derby; difficult because followers of the Fulham have such painful memories of the Baseball Ground. Super Mac's exciting team had worked hard for back-to-back promotions. In May 1982 that promotion had been achieved in a pulsating contest with Lincoln City. In May 1983 promotion was possible at 3pm but the match was abandoned at 4.32pm following repeated pitch invasions and assaults upon Fulham players. The scratching and bruising to the back of Jeff Hopkins was photographed by the hospital and offered in evidence to the courts, but all in vain. Derby were fined but the abandoned match was reinstated rather than played again at a neutral ground. Derby kept the points and thus avoided relegation; Fulham appealed but it was the close season and the authorities could not face the complications of seeing that justice was done. Malcolm Macdonald fought on but lost out and lost heart; for him (and for many followers of the Fulham) the Baseball Ground stands for all that is worst in football—crowd violence, inadequate stewarding, buck passing by the police, machinations in the boardroom, endless delays on appeals. We had to live with that end of season scandal for four awful years (viz Feet of Clay). We did not exorcise the ghosts of '83 until the Tigana teams beat Derby County year in, year out. By then, of course, the Baseball Ground had gone and few followers of the Fulham mourned its passing.

Difficult for this particular Fulhamite to be objective about the Rams because he has family and friends in Derbyshire. Three generations of Thomsons and Reeds gathered at the Baseball Ground in May 1983. Charles Reed served his time as a junior Ram. The Coppocks and the Easts are devoted to Derby County. Friendship excuses many indiscretions so I wish them well at Pride Park—especially after their generosity on and off the pitch in January 2002.

Pride Park is assuredly a magnificent stadium. Sheila was there before me. She watched Derby beat Man City when grandson Charles was a "birthday boy". I had a prior engagement at Craven Cottage and in 2002 the New Year's Day fixture was changed into an evening game. Foiled again? Frozen roads and frozen pitches but the sophisticated under-soil heating at Pride Park proved equal to the elements. Arundel Roger was happy to drive so off we went, arriving in good time and good form. Much slipping and sliding in the car park with Derek protecting his programmes and the rest of us juggling our mushy peas. The Pride Park pitch was safer than that car park and both teams attempted to play football. Christie looked more dangerous than Marlet with van der Sar having to work harder than Poom. I was preparing myself for 0–0 when a Finnan cross for Saha was deflected beyond Poom by Horacio Carbonari. Own goal and game over; we rode our luck and we counted our blessings. Come May that away win saved Fulham and did for Derby.

This is Derby's Pride Park, and this is grandson Charles as a junior Ram. Difficult to be objective about Derby.

Playgrounds Past and Playgrounds Present

You all remember your school playground and your matches of yesteryear. In the bleak midwinter of 1946–47 it was ice in the yard but game on: England v Wales. England had all the big boys and all the big names: Sandys-Lumsdaine, Temple-Morris and Barbour-Simpson. The Welsh were small boys with short names: Davies, Jones, Jones, Morgan, Morgan, Rees and Trippe. (Great name for a footballer, Trippe.) Sandys-Lumsdaine and Co did not want a Scot in their team. Thus nine years before the birth of Ivor at Merthyr and 24 years before the birth of CC at Swansea, the Welsh invited me to play against England. The English were bigger and better than us but we had the last laugh in June 1950.

Right place, right time, wrong ball... The Welsh were small boys with short names: Dai Evans, Taffy Jones and Dicky Trippe.

We observed a one-minute silence in the playground on hearing the result from Brazil (29th June 1950)—USA 1 England 0. As the captain of the USA was a Scotsman who used to play for Wrexham we had problems with this minute's silence. We took a vote. The vote was for silence but tears were optional and some of the Celts chose silent smiling. Alexander Rudolf Barbour-Simpson (headmaster) and Sandys-Lumsdaine PG (captain) were not amused. La nostalgie de la boue.

Fast forward to a larger playground beside the Thames in the 70s and 80s. Real San Paulo became the unofficial team from St Paul's with unofficial fixtures on Saturday mornings. Ivor was life president (by kind permission of Super Mac) and several of the Paulines were followers of the Fulham. Charlie Wood in goal had been acquired on a free transfer from Latymer and he was excellent. There were occasional problems with fixture congestion as Charlie had a milkround in SW6 and Craven Cottage was part of that round. Indeed Charlie's skills were known to FFC and he was called to the Cottage during an injury crisis. "Doneraile milkman stands in for Fulham." Good news for Charlie but disaster for Real San Paulo in their big match with Barnes Eagles.

School playground at Hammersmith—Real San Paulo evicted in 1968. Based at Barnes 1974 to 1984.

Come 1975 and several Paulines were out of the playground and off to Hull, Forest, Everton, Carlisle, Hillsborough, Maine Road and Wembley. They had managed to avoid the school rugby teams that winter but it all went wrong just as it was going right for Fulham. Brian Gee, Mike Anderson and Simon Borrie followed Fulham in the winter but were school cricketers in the summer. The merry month of May meant 1st XI cricket trials on Saturdays and thus the Cup Final clashed with a friendly fixture (Probables v Possibles). Brian, Mike and Simon were all Probables but Mr Hughes, the cricket coach, was not impressed with letters from home/tickets for Wembley/quiet words from PFT. Wembley won, Fulham lost, cricket lost. Brian, Mike, Simon went from 1st XI probables to 1st XI impossibles: "You'll never play for me again." Mr Hughes was obdurate and, 28 years on, Brian is resentful. Fulham never returned to Wembley and Brian never returned to St. Paul's.

Blue is the colour... The Emanuel yard contained many blue shirts. Mostly the blue of Chelsea but in the late 80s the blue of Wimbledon outnumbered the black and white of Fulham. Levesconte, Crouch, Norton, Bennett and Smythe were the last of the FFC line. A noble line which had once seen the Emanuel Sunday side playing in Fulham kit with Ron Coppock wearing number 10 and claiming that it was JH's very own shirt.

At Barnes, where I work at the Harrodian School, the playground was, once upon a time, the training ground for Ivor and Les Strong. Such names still mean something to our coach Dave Swindlehurst who knew them on and off the pitch from his days with Crystal Palace. David witnessed the grim clash between Best and Evans which left Evans with a broken leg. Fulham won the match 3–2 but Bobby Campbell and George Best let the side down by failing to visit Evans in hospital.

Match day for Harrodians. Dave Swindlehurst with his six-a-side squad. Stuart Legg (in the background) encourages the reserves.

Fulham coach on former Fulham field. Michelle Potter with her Harrodians.

Harrodians have a comfortable time of it, playing on grass or astroturf, coached by professionals—Mr Swindy for the boys, Miss Potter for the girls—both with coaching badges and ample experience. Mr Swindy from Palace but Michelle Potter from Fulham. The headmaster saw Michelle coaching in Bishop's Park and lured her to Barnes. Several pupils have been down to Motspur Park and Jack Winter, captain of the under-12s, is part of the Fulham Academy. The photograph shows Jack leading the line for Fulham against Arsenal, leading the line for a Fulham side which scored three goals against the Arsenal. Real San Paulo in 1979 gave us Dr Simon Kemp. His healing hands helped Fulham to two titles.

Wellington claimed that the battle of Waterloo was won on the playing fields of Eton. Perhaps the Intertoto campaign was won on the playgrounds of Barnes…

Jack Winter, captain of the Harrodian under-12s, leads the Fulham Academy team against Arsenal, September 2002.

Doncaster

Magnificent main stand at Doncaster—it overlooks the racecourse unlike the main stand at Belle Vue which disappeared in mysterious circumstances. Magnificent football team but they are Doncaster Belles rather than Doncaster Rovers. Magnificent social club at Doncaster but that is the council rather than the football club. This council leisure complex offers swimming, skating, bowling, squash, saunas, cinemas and snooker halls but urgent requests for partnership with the football club were rejected.

The last time I took the fast train to Doncaster the Rovers chairman was facing police charges relating to fires in the main stand while his team were at the wrong end of the third division. Fulham seemed set for the championship and an away win was confidently anticipated. We created chance after chance and called for penalty after penalty but 0–0 was the final score. That was 1997 and it was a similar story in 1982. We had won away on the Wednesday at Chester and we were sure that we could clinch promotion with victory over Rovers. Dean Coney scored in the first half but in a very rough/tough second half we were hustled into defeat. Doncaster 2 Fulham 1. Frustrated again at Doncaster.

Frustrated on the field but not off the field because the artist, the lawyer and the headmaster had enjoyed exploring the racecourse and the Dome. Doncaster has the St Leger and the Lincoln; Craven Cottage has the Boat Race and Head of the River. Rovers want a part of the Dome leisure centre and Fulham want/wanted an all purpose stadium. The Doncaster council rejected Rovers, the Hammersmith council has supported Fulham in difficult times. For the moment Fulham are in the Premiership and Doncaster have only just regained league status, but the artist, the lawyer and the headmaster have fond memories of away days at Belle Vue. Indeed for many, many years between 1968 and 2001 following the Fulham around the grounds was a heady mixture of seaside saunters and dark satanic mills/mines. For each

Doncaster racecourse— a familiar sight for fans nearing the football ground.

"Sit up, if you're going up!" Artist and artistes at the Doncaster Dome in April 1997.

and every Blackpool, Bournemouth, Brighton, Southend on Sea there was a Barnsley, Bradford, Burnley, Darlington, Doncaster, Mansfield, Rochdale.

Doncaster may be 80 places below Fulham in 2003 but in 1996 they were above us and they had won the fourth division and third division titles when we had won nothing since 1949. Doncaster's chairman had promised the fans partnership with the Dome and a £22 million development/redevelopment of Belle Vue. The chairman could not deliver the brave new stadium. New Belle Vue = paradise postponed; Old Belle Vue = paradise lost, as the main stand went up in flames.

Promises, promises, spin, spin, crisis—what crisis? Little local difficulty, fire, fire, arson? Police investigations, trial and punishment.

Same old story for Fulham fans who remember Eric Miller: promises, promises, subterfuge and suicide (September 1977). Same old story for Fulham fans who remember Ernie Clay: promises, promises, sales and more sales. Same old story for Fulham fans who remember going to Loftus Road for a season or two while Craven Cottage was redeveloped? Doncaster Dome, Greenwich Dome, Fulham Dome... In Xanadu, in Xanadu.

In Bishop's Park did Chairman Mo a stately pleasure dome decree
Where Thames, the sacred river, ran, through Craven measureless to man;
Thus riverside and ancient ground with walls and towers were girdled round...
A miracle of rare device, a sunny pleasure dome. (After Coleridge and Tennyson.)

What is it about these leisure domes and pleasure domes? Financial disasters for governments and for football clubs. The Doncaster Rovers Dome went up in smoke; the Fulham Dome is on hold. Dome on hold, home on hold—where would you rather be? Domeless or homeless? Or both?

Egaleo

Egaleo hold an extra special place in the hearts of Fulham fans because they were the last team to play a formal fixture at the old Craven Cottage. The sun was shining, there were boats on the river, there were fans in shorts just back from Costa this and Costa that, there were noisy Greeks in the Enclosure and we saw Fulham create dozens of near misses. Eventually, when we were all reconciled to another 0–0, Barry Hayles set up Louis Saha for a well worked winner. Huge sighs of relief to balance the inevitable sadness at leaving our beloved home by the river. Sheila and I paused for one long, last look across to Putney Bridge before cycling slowly back to Barnes/Mortlake via Hammersmith Bridge.

Egaleo, Egaleo—I had never even heard of you before July 2002 but now you have taken the place set aside for Everton. Anyone can write about Everton, especially Viv Busby, but only 100 supporters and the FFC squad can write about Egaleo. You who were there had fun in the sun and Chris Hatherall wrote it all up for the British press. Chris and I were the 'journalists' in Athens, though only Chris had the proper badges and the proper words. I sat at the very back of the team plane with Derek H. H for Haverhill Herald, if challenged. We were not challenged and we were very well looked after by the club officials from CEO Bruce Langham to Sarah Brookes and Liz Coley who made sure that we received the team sheets and the UEFA guidelines. There were some senior police officers who must have enjoyed the incident-free outing: "intelligence gathering". The first intelligence I gathered was that Egaleo were the Athenian equivalent to Barnet or Leyton Orient. Panathinaikos were THE team and the "ultra" of Panathinaikos had a fearsome reputation.

Egaleo play at the Karydolos stadium but it is not up to UEFA standards, hence the Intertoto fixture was set for the Panathinaikos ground. Liz

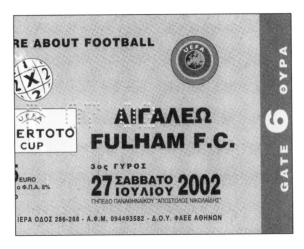

Hellish? No. Noisy? Very. Athens, 27th July 2002.

Coley had warned me that this stadium was less than elegant on the outside, hence little surprise at the rubble or graffiti. Rather more anxiety at the size of the Athenian securicor: "a measured response to the Pana 'ultra'" according to our men from the Met. Derek and I were on the coach with the club officials so we arrived with standard motor cycle escort. Once inside the ground the VIPs went one way and we joined the travelling fans in an open area with ample leg room. Meeting and greeting was closely supervised by the police and the military. The nearer we got to kick-off the greater the number of troops and the more they restricted our movement. Eighty-three followers of the Fulham were packed into one corner of the vast stadium while some 2000+ Greeks occupied the distant stand. Our 83 had at least 250 police/military/dog handlers/dog companions—and all heavily armed. My polite smile and camera were noted by the Traveller with cautionary tales from his campaign trail. We were all helpless when confronted with Radio Egaleo. Even the Greek storm troopers put their weapons down and covered their ears. Loud it was and it got even louder at half-time, but with ample cotton wool in each ear I survived.

Fulham survived after a shaky start and an Egaleo goal in the 22nd minute. Boa Morte had the beating of the Greek defence and one of his crosses was turned in by Steve Marlet just before half-time. We had many chances towards the end of the match with Goldbaek particularly impressive but 1–1 was enough. The away goal took us through (again), thank you Steve Marlet (again).

Eurostars sing and dance while The Traveller sits and prepares his statistics.

Immediately after the final whistle we were required to leave the ground, board the official coach and the police whisked us off to the airport—sirens blaring, lights flashing. The team followed some ten minutes later. No speeches, no banquets, straight onto the plane and back to Gatwick in sufficient time for Derek to make Suffolk for breakfast.

Press conference? Conducted in flight with Chris Hatherall enjoying an hour of Edwin van der Sar. I had the honour of a visit from Pugsy who was bored with Frenchmen speaking French. Sean Davis and Jon Harley opened a card school but most of the team were sleeping the sleep of the just after our second success in Europe.

The bonus of 26th and 27th July 2002 was the chance to visit/revisit Athens when most Athenians were holidaying on the islands of Aegina, Hydra and Poros. The Parthenon at sunset, the harbour by moonlight and a little gentle walking in the shade the next morning. Athens has begun to prepare for the Olympic Games but there is much yet to be done. Derek and I might return provided FFC have nothing more exciting to offer.

"Must do better" is the message from Haka; "must do better" is the message from Egaleo; but 20th July 2002 is forever memorable as the last game at Craven Cottage. Egaleo Karydolos itself I never saw (unfit for the big match). Panathinaikos? Hellish? Not really. Travelling with the team? Heavenly? A pleasure, a privilege but we left them alone and they left us alone—the days of Ivor are over. Touchez pas…silence…le genie il dorme.

Merula is Justly Jubilant on Arrival at Barnsley

"Last year the team travelled down to Barnsley on the day of play, and the tedious journey may have had some effect on our lads. Be that as it may, the directors wisely decided on this occasion to send the Cottagers as far as Sheffield on the preceding Friday. Leaving that city at midday on Saturday they arrived at Barnsley half-an-hour before the time of kicking off. All the available vehicles—two flies and a hansom—were crowded with the players. They managed to squeeze in, though, owing to the huge bulk of Carter, the reserve man, it was a tight fit.

"The directors had to thread their way afoot, but, lest they should be dull, the courteous locals greeted the "foreigners" with genial yells of "Six to nothing"—that being the score by which Fulham lost there last year. I attribute these amenities to the *entente-cordiale*. French politeness and charm of manner are evidently permeating even the Yorkshire mining districts.

"The entrances and offices of the Barnsley Club have been much improved, but the playing arena, so interesting to visitors, had unfortunately been left unaltered. That is deplorable, for the touch lines are so close to the railings as to disconcert visitors, and to be positively dangerous. Moreover, the corner kick has to be taken practically standing. Besides being cramped for space, the ground has an uneven surface, so that the total peculiarities of the field are a real handicap to strangers.

"These topographical details are given, not by way of complaint, but to emphasise the value of the Cottagers' victory."

From "The Cottagers' Journal",
5th December 1908

Could that be Merula reading words of wisdom to his bonny boys?

Fulham

There were other grounds between 1879 and 1896 and there may well be other grounds after Loftus Road, but Fulham's ground is Craven Cottage. Fans may follow the Fulham over land and sea, but home, sweet home is down by the riverside at Craven Cottage.

In July 2002 Patrick Mascall masterminded a handsome publication *Celebrating Craven Cottage* just as we were packing our bags for Loftus Road. 190 pages and many illustrations seek to do justice to our beloved home.

Celebrating Craven Cottage. From page 116: "Picture the scene. The tide is high and so is the sun. The Thames sparkles and a dozen yachts dance off the Hammersmith End. Which other football ground offers such a dazzling setting in bleak mid-winter?"—PFT, New Year's Day, 1995.

What is there to add to *Celebrating Craven Cottage*? Thanks to Ken Coton and unknown photographer, words are superfluous. Let the four photos opposite do the talking: Game on…Goal from Haynes; Going to the Match; Celebrating at Craven Cottage; Sitting by the River.

Grimsby

Nothing grim about Grimsby; well, nothing grim about Grimsby once you get there. It takes hours by road, even when you start off in Lincolnshire. Kirton to Boston to Skegness to Louth to Cleethorpes equals 2½ hours if you're lucky. Tricky old trip by train and a very long slog in Mary Doughty's coach. Stay the night in Lincolnshire if you possibly can and enjoy the sands at Cleethorpes. Famous fish and friendly folk but don't expect fine wine. After the play-offs in May 1998 (when the ten men of Fulham just lost out) a robust vintage was requested. "No call for red wine in Grimsby." Red cards—yes; red wine—no.

"Ken, Ken, did you get the goals?" He didn't in January in 1954: Grimsby 5 Fulham 5 (though he was there as a non camera-carrying fan). He missed out in November 1982 when Fulham went to play a Grimsby side which had just beaten Leeds. Confident they may have been at 3pm but they were blown away by Gale force Fulham. The 4–0 final score sounds good but it could have been six or seven. The Grimsby cross bar was their busiest defender and years afterwards their programme notes did homage to Ray Houghton's passing and running. The Dutch may have invented total football but any follower of Fulham will tell you that we were totally sublime that autumn afternoon. Sheila, ever generous, suggested that it might have been fun if Grimsby had scored one. They did in September 1983. One too many; despite an early goal from Ivor we were done 2–1. That match was a bad day out for Fulham and a worse day out for the Thomsons. An early morning training run ended up in the doctor's surgery. Sheila was lumbered with all the driving to Cleethorpes and back. I can just about remember Ivor's goal but I was too ill to watch the second half.

We were all under the weather in November 1984. Ivor had scored against Wimbledon but was sold off to Chelsea—Super Mac's million dollar man allowed to go to Stamford Bridge for much less than the £300,000 asking price. Desolate we took the long, long road to Cleethorpes and desolate we watched Grimsby take an early lead. Wet and windy, bitterly cold and a thrashing on the cards—but who is that emerging from the mud and the mist? "Leroy, Leroy, give us a goal!" And he did, and he did, and he did. Hat-trick hero helps Fulham to splendid 4–2 victory. Le roi est mort, vive le roi. King Ivor is dead, long live Leroy. Nothing grim about Grimsby that November.

Nothing grim about Grimsby in November 1987. I flew back from the New York marathon in time for Fulham 5 Grimsby 0. Ivor was back with us again, of course, and Ivor scored for us again, of course.

New Year's Day 1991: Sheila and I were in Lincolnshire but bad vibes and bad weather forced us off the Skegness road. We turned south and missed a miserable performance and a 3–0 defeat.

Ice, snow and the orange ball in January 1998 (1–1). We had the four fixtures with Grimsby that season and failed to win any of them but November 2000 saw Boa Morte and Saha set up victory in our season of seasons. We were first division champions with 101 points when we set out for Cleethorpes in May 2001. The sun was shining, there were parties on the beach, nothing grim about Grimsby (we had brought our own red wine). Right wine, wrong goalkeeper. Marcus O.G. Hahnemann had gifted a goal to Wednesday in April and gifted another to Grimsby in May. Always a mistake to leave out/ loan out Maik Taylor. Grimsby avoided relegation and we may well meet them again. I hope so. There's nothing grim about Grimsby.

Grimsby versus Fulham, November 1984. The programme features Kevin Moore—now a Motspur man— receiving his Mariner's Player of the Month award. He captains his team to a 4–2 defeat.

MARINER MAN

Martell 'Player of the Month' Kevin Moore receives his gallon of Martell Brandy from Mr Bryan Jarvis of Tates Ltd.

Haka

H is for Haka and for Hatch and for Hatherall. Steven Hatch and Chris Hatherall are good companions from the Intertoto tour. The former is Fulham through and through, the latter supports Brentford but he is the only journalist to have reported on every single fixture from Haka home and away in July to Berlin and back in December.

The Hatch photograph from Finland shows the whites playing in black. Note the Haka VIP area—a bowling green shed beneath the trees. The tea tents at Macclesfield come to mind and given the date (14th July) the summery

scene suits this summer game. The Hatherall report hints at the fragility of our performance and it took Marlet's away goal to carry us through to the next round. Marlet has struggled in the Premiership but his record overseas is impressive. Without his five goals there would have been little to celebrate in Europe.

Followers of the Fulham are inclined to bemoan a lack of luck over the years: the own goal which cost us the final of the Anglo-Scottish Cup, the injury to Les Strong on the eve of the FA Cup final, the abandoned match at Derby in May 1983, etc, etc, but at Haka we had all the luck that was going.

Mr Tigana was quick to admit that Fulham were fortunate to go through to the next round. Chairman Mohamed Al Fayed and Heini, his Finnish wife, did not make their views known to the press but Haka was not what most of us envisaged when we qualified for the Intertoto tournament. Bologna…that's more like it. Split, Zagreb and Berlin…now you're talking Europe, and what fun we had at those major international grounds. Agreed but only thanks to Marlet and Lady Luck who carried us over the Haka hurdle.

Hereford

Chester, Exeter, Hereford, Lincoln, Norwich, Oxford and York are cathedral cities with football grounds, thus for culture vultures ideal spots for long week-ends of football plus. In Blairspeak, a visit to Hereford is "value added" following of the Fulham.

From the Len Weston stand at Edgar Street you can gaze out on the cattle market, the cider mill, the cathedral and the green, green hills beyond. Treasures such as the chained library and the Mappa Mundi make the cathedral a must for medievalists. Cider may not be required drinking for followers of the Fulham but Hereford's riverside pubs are the equal of our *Crabtree*, *Rutland* or *Dove*. Oarsmen can attempt the three local regattas: Hereford, Monmouth and Worcester.

The most famous of all Hereford's many matches was the FA Cup tie with Newcastle in 1972. Fulham legends Busby and Macdonald were playing for the Magpies and Super Mac scored from a Busby cross but 'Rocket' Ronnie Radford hit a 40-yarder which (like Harley v Villa) has become a collector's item on TV and video. A less distinguished nudge from Ricci George gave Hereford the victory 2–1.

Hereford's cup tie with Fulham in 1982 was memorable for reasons other than the goal of the game. Fulham were going well in the league with a 14 match unbeaten run plus two victories over Newcastle in the League Cup. Our FA Cup game with Hereford fell victim to ice and snow with postponement after postponement which made it difficult to book leisurely long

De consolatione philosophiae. *After the mud and muck of Edgar Street, January 1982, solace and sanctuary were available at Hereford cathedral. Comfort for the vanquished—a medieval ivory from 1150.*

week-ends. Finally a thaw made play possible at Edgar Street and I set out in the mini with Nick and Charles Wood as map readers and companions. The pitch was heavy, very heavy, and Fulham were never in the contest. We lost a miserable game to a miserable goal and drove back in the dark. What a contrast with September '76 when Marsh and Best danced in the sun at Craven Cottage—Fulham 4 Hereford 1, and all five goals scored by FFC.

Sunshine also at Edgar Street in 1997 with Fulham set fair for promotion. An 11 game unbeaten run was never endangered by Hereford but Conroy and McAree had packed their shooting boots for Carlisle so a pleasant day out became a bit of a no-score bore.

We have not been back to Hereford for football as our league fortunes have differed, with Hereford in the Conference and Fulham in the Premiership. Perhaps the FA Cup will call us back to Edgar Street for cider with Rosie and rockets from Ron.

Trains and Planes

For years and years it was the train taking the strain when Fulham were playing 'somewhere up north'. Up north to Peterborough in under an hour and York in under two hours—no strain. Up north (well, north-east) to Norwich or to Ipswich—once again fast train meant no strain. Sometimes there was hardly time to start moaning about last week's performance before the train had pulled into Peterborough or Colchester or Ipswich. Returning from Chesterfield in 1994 there was a mad dash from ground to station. The referee penalised Chesterfield for time wasting and Kevin Moore scrambled a goal in the 96th minute but there was hardly a moment to celebrate the late, late equaliser for fear of missing the Topley special.

Mind you, if it was 'somewhere up north'—Blackpool via Preston or Stoke via Crewe or Mansfield via Nottingham—then it was far from simple. Involved were long, cold waits on long, cold benches because the small, warm waiting-rooms were full. If it was an evening game those small warm waiting-rooms would be locked and the milk train would be running late. Many the November night we had to change at Crewe while Mary Doughty counted her flock. Talk about the good shepherd: Mary rescuing naughty youngsters from local constables; Mary talking us through dubious penalty decisions, obvious off-side goals given against us, brilliant Fulham efforts disallowed by 'homer' referees and linesmen; Mary comforting us when we were crashing out of the promotion places; Mary reassuring us that we would bounce back next year when we faced the drop (again). Ivor recorded how greatly he valued Mary's happy band of pilgrims. Hooray for Mary! I hope that she has enjoyed recent promotions. Mary deserves a blue plaque from British Rail and a gold plaque from FFC.

In the Adams, Keegan, Tigana years the trains have been organised by the patron saint of travellers, Saint Christopher. Top man Topley has done us proud. Mary had tired teams on the pitch but worked with good old British Rail. Chris has quality teams running around the grounds but suffers from tired old trains on tired old tracks. I remember some hysterical delays and detours on the way to Blackpool with electric faults and power failures but Chris got us there for snow on the beach and waves breaking over the top of our double decker bus. There was another nightmare journey in 2001 when the Topley special just about made the second half at Hillsborough. The players responded and turned one goal down into a thrilling 3–3. Chris has got us into the Premiership with a smile and he too deserves plaques from Virgin Railways. Never mind Sir Richard, what about Sir Christopher?

The very best train to carry FFC freight around the grounds was chartered by our chairman in April 2002. Off to Villa Park in a posh, plush Pullman car with real wooden tables, velvet cushions and little gilt lamps with little gilt lampshades. Travel in style, play like drains, lose a nothing game to a nothing goal—FA Cup semi-final on the wrong day at the wrong time. The cup game at York was much more fun but at last and at least we left Villa Park on the same lovely train. My son-in-law could sleep away the pain while I found myself deep in conversation with two total strangers from the Hammersmith End. How could I have missed them 1951–2002? They had seen Haynes and Robson, Cohen and Keetch, all the good old boys from the good old days. By the time we had cursed Clay and Bulstrode, laughed over Dicks and Och Aye Don, the train had reached London and somehow the worst of the day had been talked away. We were reconciled and ready to face mouldy Monday morning with those office mockers who had watched it all on TV. To drive back via gridlocked motorways would have been too, too terrible. Let the train take the strain. It did on the night of 4 April 2002. Thank you, chairman.

By way of a diversion I reprint here the railway thoughts of Fulham fan Steven Hatch, which he entitles *Awaydays*.

My two passions in life are watching Fulham and being a railway enthusiast, and travelling to away games gives me an opportunity to combine both interests. I have fond memories of many rail trips around the country following the Whites. When I first got seriously into attending away games around the 94–95 season, every other weekend the same handful of faces would appear at Euston or King's Cross, and although I didn't know their names everyone always spoke. At that time there were few people going to games in the third division and the fans' relationship was more personal.

If I look back at the history of the 'Football Special' I missed out on the golden era by around 15 years! Back in the seventies even mundane games in the north would have warranted a charter train; the MK 1 rolling stock provided would be a wreck but football hooligans hardly encouraged British Rail to use anything better. The engines that worked these trains would be interesting because of their rarity in passenger use, and even obscure stations like Boothferry Park at Hull were still open. I doubt that the football fan of the 1970s appreciated any of this but to a modern enthusiast a lot of these charters are of great interest. Sadly BR pulled out from this operation to save money and also because they got fed up with repairing the carriages!

September 1975—those were the days. Football specials ran to Boothferry Park, allowing railwaymen to watch John Mitchell putting his best foot forward.

Nowadays, although a few football specials still run, most of my travelling is on service trains. Over the nine years that I have followed Fulham away from the Cottage there have been some memorable journeys. These include being stuck at Newton Abbot when a Fulham fan locked the guard inside his van; being marooned at Gainsborough Lea Road when our Sprinter train ran out of coolant; watching in horror whilst the driver read his paper as he drove his train from Huddersfield to Wakefield; and taking six hours to reach Preston when the west coast was suffering from speed restrictions. But the highlight for me was the semi-final charter to Villa Park for the Chelsea match. If the carriages had been painted blue and grey it could have been 1975 all over again...

But FLY to football? Ridiculous! Only stars of stage and screen do that. David Hamilton had to take a plane from the studio to reach Manchester in time for the FA Cup semi-final replay in 1975. Fair enough—but ordinary followers of the Fulham? Surely not. Then I hear that Hammersmith Enders are flying to Newcastle for the promotion cruncher with Carlisle in 1997. Next it's Arundel Roger celebrating the Premiership with flights to Newcastle for the Sunderland match in January in 2002.

Nothing wrong with trains, say I—until the summer of 2002. Suddenly it's all aboard the team plane for Athens—great fun—but back to the train for Sochaux. Good old train taking the strain but also taking its time—6am to 6.20pm and a sprint to make the ground for the kick-off. (Buzz Air to Dijon was half the price and very much quicker.) Sheila and I then find ourselves flying to Bologna and Split. True, Dave Pearce drove there but not without great difficulty and no little danger.

Berlin by rail? Possible but not much chance of working that week if you take the train. Anyway, haven't you had your quota of weeks off this year? Fly in and out for half the rail fare and one-eighth of the time. Done and dusted; we all meet at Berlin's Olympic Stadium at 5pm and we are all back at our desks the next morning. Euroflight for UEFA—you know it makes sense.

Ipswich

Ipswich and Fulham are bound together by Bobby Robson. Robson scored for Fulham on Boxing Day 1963 when Ipswich were beaten 10–1. Robson was with Fulham from 1950 to 1956 and from 1962 to 1967. He scored 80 goals for Fulham before turning to management. Ten months at Craven Cottage followed by 13 happy years at Portman Road. "I was out of work after being sacked by Fulham and I needed a break. Ipswich gave me that break."

From an Ipswich programme of 2002, looking back to Robson's managership.

Fancy Dans from London SW may look upon Suffolk as sleepy and remote East Anglia but the roll of honour at Portman Road includes the league championship in 1961–62, the FA Cup in 1978 and the UEFA Cup in 1981. That roll of honour deserves an impressive home and the Portman Road which we visited in January 2002 was assuredly impressive. I got there early and enjoyed my tour of the stadium. Later I was the guest of Richard Ryder in the board room where a bulging trophy cabinet and four-star catering eased the pain which was to follow. Wind and rain lashed the players while George Burley reminded his team of the need for urgent action after FA Cup humiliation: Ipswich 1 Manchester City 4. Fulham were confident/overconfident after a less testing cup tie at Bootham Crescent: York City 0 Fulham 2.

Ipswich were quicker, more determined and more positive. Marcus Bent scored early and might have added other goals before half-time. Fulham offered little and I made my apologies at the final whistle. A brisk walk to the railway station and the fast train back to London rather than the traditional courtesy of the board room.

Ipswich had beaten us and went on to complete a convincing double over Spurs—surely they were far too good to go down. On the evidence of

Portman Road, it was Fulham who were about to lose their Premiership status. I was down in the dumps after such an inept performance, altogether unworthy of the occasion, the mighty stadium and the generous hospitality of the Ipswich directors.

MR P THOMSON

IPSWICH TOWN FOOTBALL CLUB

BOARDROOM PASS

IPSWICH TOWN V FULHAM.

2001/2002
ADMIT ONE

DRESS CODE APPLIES

Come April 2002 we survived thanks to gutsy performances at Newcastle and Leeds. Ipswich were every ounce as gutsy but their opponents in April and May were Arsenal, Manchester United and Liverpool. European adventures in 2001, relegation in 2002, financial crisis in 2003…Ipswich deserved and deserve better. Fulham beware, Fulham be warned.

Jerudong Park—the Ground that Got Away

J is for jolly—jolly difficult. I asked my publisher if phonetics could be exploited here with Gillingham as "Jillingham" but he said no and I was somewhat relieved. Gillingham and the Priestfield stadium have too many bad memories for too many Fulham fans. The battle of Priestfield in 1995 and the murder of Matthew Fox in 1998 were the very worst examples of recent tension at Gillingham, but I gave up on the Priestfield in December 1994. An FA Cup match ended 1–1 on the pitch but some of Mary Doughty's most vulnerable companions were pushed and shoved by Gillingham stewards and the local police waved away all requests for help.

Thus, if J is not for "Jillingham" and Fulham have not been in action at (St) Johnstone, some ingenuity is required. Jerudong Park is off the beaten track for most followers of the Fulham but not for Kevin Keegan, Peter Beardsley and Peter Thomson. We all went there to promote football and in various ways we all worked there on behalf of Fulham. Some of us were wearing Fulham colours most of the time and others were promoting the Fulham cause behind closed doors. In February 1997 Bill Muddyman gave me an SOS call as I set out for Borneo to MC a football tournament at Jerudong Park. Ian Branfoot was working on Keegan and Beardsley who were playing in that tournament. Keegan, Beardsley, Bracewell and I hosted the Sultan's nephew at Craven Cottage and some of this bonding was due to result in a fixture in July 2003 when FFC, Spurs and Liverpool were scheduled to meet the Brunei national team in a tournament at Jerudong.

> *I dreamt that I dwelt in marble halls*
> *With vassals and serfs at my side...*

At Jerudong the halls are more marble, much more marble than at Highbury. There are vassals and serfs on every side to see that Fulham's senior citizens are not jostled as they make their way to the banquet after the match.

JT had wanted more Intertoto travel for Fulham. Sheila and I have done the Intertoto tour but we were very ready to return to Jerudong with Fulham. Instead we went off to Torquay and Livingston with CC. For followers of the Fulham, Jerudong Park remains the ground that got away.

From left: Ryder Cup captain and golf coach Bernard Gallacher; a welcome note from Kevin Keegan to Prince Bahar on a visit to Craven Cottage; Prince Hakeem—marksman and Olympic athlete (Atlanta and Sydney) and most generous host 1987–97.

Kenilworth Road

Luton Town—famous for hats, Vauxhall motors, Eric Morecambe, Lorraine Chase and her airport. Luton Town—infamous for that plastic pitch covered in seats hurled there by the rioters of Millwall in 1985.

Luton's links with Fulham are cosier than those with Millwall. Three Fulham legends graduated from Kenilworth Road. Alec Stock, Viv Busby and Alan Slough took us all the way to Wembley. Since the Cup Final our visits to Luton have included some real treats such as Rodney Marsh returning to the scoresheet in September '76 and a hat-trick from Paul Moody in January '98. Luton caught us cold at the Cottage in October '98 but we overwhelmed them 4–0 at Kenilworth Road and beat them there again in an FA Cup replay in December '99.

Alan Slough left Kenilworth Road for Craven Cottage in 1973. Went all the way to Wembley in 1975. Club captain from 1976 to 1977.

Luton pioneered plastic pitches in 1985 and quickly added the ban on away fans—mad as hatters those Hatters. They maintained their customary eccentricity when they converted the far end into seating for visitors in 1986. You enter via the back gardens of terraced houses and climb steps into what must have been bedrooms before squeezing into the most uncomfortable seats I have ever encountered. Loftus Road's seats are bad for anyone over 6 foot tall but the chamber of horrors at Kenilworth Road tortures all those over 5 foot 2 inches.

It is difficult to believe that a little club like Luton could survive in the top flight for ten seasons and win the League Cup in 1988 (Luton 3 Arsenal 2) but they did and they did it under former Fulham coach and manager Ray Harford. There must be a lesson here for us—we are a little club mixing it in the Premiership. We are unlikely to become "the Manchester United of the south" despite the aspirations and investments of Mr Al Fayed.

Eric Morecambe took the Hatters into the big time and *Bring Me Sunshine* was his anthem. Alec Stock brought us some of that sunshine when he joined us from Kenilworth Road. He died in the knowledge that Fulham were champions of the first division. I hope he is working with those spirits of J block to bring the sunshine back to the Cottage.

Road Rage

"Without a ruck it wasn't a good day out…" Thought for the day from Newport as Alex Ferguson faced up to the 'buckos from the boozer'. See chapter 36 of *Pandora's Fulhamish Box* for details of those 'battered' in August 1973.

Battered I was not, but there were awkward incidents aplenty in the 70s. Chelsea, Leeds, Man Utd used to be tricky but are much improved since Heysel, Hillsborough and the Taylor report. Birmingham, Burnley, Cardiff and Millwall remain unsavoury. If you ask for trouble at those grounds you will probably get it, but outside the famous four (plus UEFA hotspots Croatia and Turkey) there is relatively little road rage nowadays.

All very different from the 70s when we were ambushed by Baggies and by Barnsley. Mary Doughty had her coaches rocked at Bolton. A supporters bus had windows smashed by young kids near Everton. There was even an incident at Clapham Junction when traditionally placid Charlton fans piled into us as we took the underpass from platform 11 to platform 5.

Typical of those distant and difficult days was a confrontation at Euston station. In the black and white corner an ancient Fulham fan; in the blue corner several youngsters from Chelsea. Salty Jones of FFC had fought in both world wars and was justly proud of his days at sea. The loudmouthed yobs from the Bridge were cautioned by Salty on the need for courtesy, consideration and the manners which maketh man. Outnumbered, outflanked but not outranked Salty listened patiently to another load of insults before advancing on the largest Shedender. "Where were you in the Blitz? When were you last torpedoed?" Long pause while the Blues looked at little old Salty. Eventually the reply: "Torpedo, torpedo—never met a torpedo—but we was well bricked at Burnley."

In May 1973 I saw a Portsmouth fan fight off four Oxford thugs with a heavy belt in one hand and light trousers in the other. Salty Jones retained his trousers and his dignity while upholding the good name of Fulham.

Phil—"upholding the good name of Fulham". Dedicated follower of fashion—from the 70s. Home and away with FFC throughout the 70s. Still going strong with Fulham in 2003. Norwegian based season ticket holder.

Lincoln City

Ken Coton's famous photograph of Roger Brown's goal in May 1982 has pride of place on my walls, next to Jason Bowyer's "Hammersmith End". The Brown goal set up promotion for Fulham and frustrated Lincoln. Fulham were promoted, Lincoln stagnated and were relegated. In 1987 Lincoln fell into the Vauxhall Conference while Fulham settled for 18th place in the third division. Lincoln bounced back and then bounced all over Fulham home and away: five consecutive defeats for FFC including a Lincoln 'double' over the Micky Adams promotion team.

The city of Lincoln, as opposed to Lincoln City, is immensely impressive. Ancient cobbled streets lead up the hill to the cathedral. Rebuilt in Gothic style in 1185 this vast and vastly impressive monument to Hugh of Lincoln's faith is well worth 45 minutes each way. 45 minutes climbing the hill and walking the cloisters, 45 minutes within admiring a medieval stadium of light. Make sure you find the Lincoln imp which was adopted by the football club. Followers of the Fulham back in September 1981 were pleased to meet up with Les Strong in the cathedral: a precious point at Sincil Bank that afternoon. 1–1 in front of 3,034 in September followed by 1–1 in front of 20,398 at the Cottage in May. Honours even that season but not in 1995–96.

Boxing Day 1995, and up early to check the weather: snow in the air, snow on the ground and more snow to follow. Sheila and I were staying with relatives at Kirton in Lincolnshire, thus a local call to Sincil Bank just to confirm that the match had been postponed. Postponed? Far from it, the pitch inspection suggested that play would be possible. Possible for penguins presumably because when I reached Lincoln it was still snowing and freezing fast. With every possible extra garment on plus blankets over my shoulder it was straight to the ground, no time for the cathedral. Simon Morgan and Ian Branfoot were engaged in a lively conversation with the referee. Thamesbank travellers from the 70s assured me that the match was off. Wrong; the Imps got their skates on and were 2–0 ahead by half-time. Morgs was moaning but the referee was deaf/blind to such courtesies. The Thamesbank experts were wired for sound and they brought confirmation that the match had been abandoned. Wrong again, because Lincoln raced out for the second half while Morgs and Branfoot pleaded with the ref. All in vain, all in vain, Lincoln City score again and again. Final score: Lincoln 4 Fulham 0. For a player's eye view, turn to page 50 of *On Song for Promotion*.

Sincil Bank, Boxing Day 1995. Weather bad, football worse.

Simon wrote: "I can honestly say that only once in my Fulham career have I ever knowingly given less than 100%. That was on a ridiculously icy surface at Lincoln one Boxing Day. I found it difficult even to stand up that day and an elbow to the face that needed two stitches was the final straw."

Miserable afternoon on the pitch and miserable afternoon off it—a long, slow drive with the windscreen wipers working overtime to deal with the snow. My journey took under two hours but that was across Lincolnshire; goodness knows when the Fulham faithful reached SW6. Boxing Day blues and 90th in the Nationwide League. It could only get better in March when Lincoln came to the Cottage. Well, it did, in that "Ooh, Rodney, Rodney" McAree scored a goal—but the Imps scored twice and took the points.

Micky Adams and the Muddymans saved Fulham but Old Fulham always struggled against Lincoln City. Cometh the Keegan, cometh the Beardsley, cometh long overdue victories at Sincil Bank 2–1 and at the Cottage 1–0.

Still far from easy, but job done. Fulham ended the season on 101 points and were champions; Lincoln with 46 points were relegated.

Lincoln can't kick Fulham off the park at Loftus Road but the Imps can still ruin my dreams. It is May 18th 1982 again and we are still screaming for the final whistle. Time added on and time added on. Lincoln score and they go up.

Lincoln, Lincoln—more incubus than imp.

Make sure you visit Lincoln Cathedral—a medieval stadium of light. Note the Lincoln Imp, city emblem since 1888.

Groundsmen and Groundswomen
1921–2001

Take a look at this team photo from 1921. Mr Walker (at far left) is next to Mr Dean, thus groundsman and director stand shoulder to shoulder at Craven Cottage. Take a look at the photo below from 2001—Mr Frank Senior and Mr Muddyman, groundsman and director, side by side again at the Cottage, just as it should be. A team's as good as the ground and the ground's as good as the groundsman.

I never met Mr Walker but Mr Magee and I walked together, talked together and occasionally worked together from 1981 to 1995. Walking together and talking together mainly at Craven Cottage. We were supposed to be training for the London marathon so I would run from Barnes Bridge to the ground and we would chat about FFC.

I would then run back to Barnes Bridge while the mighty Magee put together his own unbroken run of 730 matches following the Fulham home and away. Good for Steve, good for Fulham, but bad for his marathon training. When FFC were prospering on the pitch (as they assuredly were 1981–83), running for promotion and running for marathons meant daily visits to the Cottage. Wise words from Magee and a chance to read the match reports which were scrawled upon the walls of the boiler room. Before the invention of clubcalls and internets the Magee grapevine was both informed and informative.

Payback came in January and February 1982 when ice and snow had to be removed from the pitch. Those seeking the truth about Ivor's injury or manager of the month awards had to earn their updates. Shovel that snow, fill that barrow, scrape ice from that terrace; work well and you could thaw out in the boiler room while reading what Les Strong thought of Lock's goal at Swindon. If you worked especially hard Magee might take you up to the manager's office where there were chocolate biscuits. From 28th November 1981 to 30th January 1982 the Fulham pitch was frozen. No football at Craven Cottage for two months despite the best efforts of Magee and his acolytes. Eventually we did get the ice off the terraces and Ivor celebrated with that astonishing goal against Chesterfield, scored, it seemed, from inside Magee's corner flag/office/boiler room.

Magee moved on to mastermind the travels of London Broncos but every now and again he calls on the men of '82. Appropriately (mid blizzard) there was Magee in February 2002 rejoining Fulham fans on the way to Highbury.

Ian Branfoot brought Frank to Craven Cottage. Frank had been with Reading first as a player then as a groundsman. Magee had trained as a painter/decorator but Frank has formal qualifications and diplomas in horticulture. Some fans think the departure of the rugby league team improved our playing surface, others credit Frank with truer pitches in the championship years.

Ten years before Magee placed the first of many corner flags Fulham recruited Yvonne and Sandra. The former served the club for 20 years, the latter is still with us, patiently restoring order to the ticket office. Yvonne and Sandra saw Fulham through many administrative difficulties and provided devoted support at away games for more than 30 years. Turn to page 124 of *Fulham Photos* and you will see the golden girls on the bench for FFC. Turn to page 83 of *Following the Fulham* and you will see them enjoying an away game at Cambridge. Home and away we have been very well served by our groundsmen and our groundswomen.

This is Sandra in 1979, parcelling up the centenary history books. She has now (in 2003) completed thirty years with Fulham, a milestone suitably commemorated by the club.

Craven Cottage is a garden that is full of stately views ...
But the glory of that garden lies in more than meets the eye.

Craven Cottage is a garden and such gardens are not made
By singing "Oh, how beautiful" and sitting in the shade.
Steve, Frank, Yvonne and Sandra devoted working lives
To grubbing weeds from Cottage paths with broken dinner knives.

Oh, Adam was a gardener and God who made him sees
That half a proper gardener's work is done upon his knees;
So when your work is finished, you can wash your hands and pray
For the glory of the Cottage, that it may not pass away!

Thanks to Steve, Frank, Yvonne and Sandra it did not pass away,
The glory of the Cottage, it shall never pass away...

Kiplingish tribute to our groundsmen and groundswomen.

Livingston

Last but not least—Livingston. Last, because a copy date of 6th August meant just that, a 'deadline'. Deadlines are honoured at Ashwater Press. Not least, because Livingston beat us fair and square. Younger, fitter, faster, they were well worth their two-goal lead at half-time. Enter Dean Leacock to transform the second half but we failed to score. The 100+ travelling fans could not question the result although there were reservations (and songs) about a goalkeeper who is older than Jim Stannard. "*Rip Van Beasant in our goal! Doodah, doodah...*" Livingston, as I said, were younger, fitter, faster.

Not least Livingston because we have much to learn from the Lions of West Lothian. They, like us, roared through the lower divisions to reach the SLP. In 2002 they, like us, qualified for Europe. Ten years ago they were relegated to the second division and pre-seasoned at Clachnacuddin; now in the SLP they face Celtic and Rangers. In August 1996 we were pre-seasoning at Ballygar and now we are in the Premiership with the Arsenal and Man United. So why should we be learning from our cousins at the Almondvale City Stadium?

Livingston used to be Meadowbank Thistle, based at the athletics stadium in Edinburgh. Their sponsor, Bill Hunter, urged them to relocate to survive, relocate to prosper, relocate to dream the dream. "My aim is to see us in the Premiership. People may laugh but if you don't set your sights on achieving the very best, then there's no point in being in the game." In reply *The Thistle* pointed to the decline in support from a healthy

Livingston, I presume. Old friend, new ground—Steve at the Almondvale City Stadium in August 2003.

900 to a dismal 200 who had no intention of following Hunter to the 'Livi lavvypan'.

Thistle supporters regarded the move to a new town with the same loathing as Dons view Milton Keynes and Fulham question anything other than Craven Cottage. Hunter and Jim Leishman were ridiculed as they worked for the change of ground and change of name. Now they have their own compact modern stadium with four training pitches. Now they are established in the SLP.

Of course we want to return to the Cottage but if that is not possible we must learn from others—not least Livingston.

Last point about Livingston. Who welcomed us on our arrival at their ground? Saviour of the club and architect of four promotions: Jim Leishman. How was our journey? Any news of Jimmy Hill? Did we remember two of his former players—Doug Rougvie and John Watson?" Alex the Traveller and I were effusive in our tributes to Rougvie and fastidiously selective in our comments on Watson, J. We could not be other than deferential to the darling of Dunfermline and lion of Livingston—Jim 'The Legend' Leishman, a Scottish version of Alec Stock, a gentle genius, a lovely man.

Motspur Park

Ruxley Lane, Barn Elms, Lonsdale Road, Raynes Park, Bank of England, Fire Brigade fields—we have trained here and there. Many the "barren and windswept waste" described by Simon Morgan and many the less than enthusiastic training session observed by one man and his dog.

All change for Motspur Park and all change at Motspur Park—space and grace, an academy of excellence, all the latest medical equipment and all the latest sports science. Alan Smith and his youth scheme, Chris Smith and his physio regime, Roger Propos and the French school of fitness…all supported Damiano and Tigana as they prepared their squad for the season of seasons 2000–01.

"Flying start" was an article in *Cottage Pie* which attempted to show the new methods and the new mood at Motspur Park. The next season *Cottage Pie* sent me back to interview Bonetti on Taylor and Taylor on Bonetti.

Safety first. Kevin Moore leads the chairman around our Motspur Park training ground. July 1998.

Somewhere in between there was a training session with Sean Davis. Well, he trained and I took photographs. Towards the end of Burley's time at Ipswich there was a friendly fixture at Motspur Park with positive comments from their manager and directors. Spring 2003 and the Japanese press (and the Japanese schoolgirls) wait patiently for Inamoto. All so very, very different from training sessions behind the cemetery at Putney Vale where Och Aye Don's doomed squad slow motioned through the mud.

Mr Al Fayed's Craven Cottage is incomplete but Motspur Park is magnificent. "Si monumentum requiris circumspice." If you seek his memorial look around you; in Surrey he has a Premiership training ground; by the river he has the remains of the Cottage.

How many of these 1999 internationals, photographed at Motspur Park, can you recognise? Only two—Chris Coleman and Simon Morgan—are still with the club.

Around the Grounds by Coach

Mary Doughty was queen of the road for at least 25 years and there is a story/legend/myth that at least two of her younger charges/proteges/junior black and whites later graduated to become directors and saviours of Fulham in 1987.

I enjoyed many away days with Mary and Barbara Doughty in the 1970s and was once appointed bus monitor for a trip to Stoke. On arrival my reward was a free seat in the VIP area next to Sue Davies. Mrs Davies was loud in her condemnation of Peter Kitchen who had just become our record signing and (albeit briefly) threatened Ivor's place on the team sheet.

Far and away my favourite coach journey was that mid-week trip to Mansfield when we finally climbed out of the bargain basement and secured our first promotion for 15 years. We didn't have any champagne on our coach but Will and Bea Guard made teas and coffees to keep the songsters singing.

Worst of all…well, there was the driver who crossed his Cs and took us to Cambridge rather than Colchester. Then there was the Bescot breakdown which put three hours on the return trip, and motorway gridlocks which involved watching a cup game on Sky at Uttoxeter rather than at Anfield. Never mind, the prices have been consistently reasonable and latterly more than generous—thank you, chairman.

The major snag with a club coach is the tight schedule; thus motorway service stations by the dozen but very few castles, cathedrals, museums or beach football and trips round the bay.

Clive Walker arrives at Meadow Lane (signed picture). His goal enabled 10-man Fulham to beat Notts County, 29th October 1988.

Norwich City

Norwich City—a happy hunting ground for followers of the Fulham. Mitchell scored twice in March 1975 thus completing the good work begun by Busby at Craven Cottage back in September (Fulham 4 Norwich 0). In 1999 we were excellent at Carrow Road in the Worthington Cup winning 4–0 and we won again in the league fixture with goals from Riedle and Hayles.

So much for the football, now please consider the fringe benefits of following the Fulham to Norwich. Within easy walking distance of the railway station you have a cathedral, the university of East Anglia, a castle, a museum, a major art gallery and a brewery. Within (easy?) running distance you have the Norfolk coast—Kelling, Cley and Cromer. You don't have to run from the coast to Carrow Road (although it can be done in 3 hours and 31 minutes); you can drive the 26 miles in under the hour, or take a little longer via Southwold/Jason Bowyer's country cottage/the Bungay brewery.

Norwich City was good news back in '74–'75 and it is even better news now that Delia Smith has taken over the Carrow Road catering. Four- and five-star food at the football ground in August 2000 plus a well timed winner from Luis Boa Morte.

In addition to Delia Smith, Norwich City has Horatio Nelson. On the backstairs of this riverside hotel, we bumped into Jean Tigana and the French contingent that August Bank Holiday. There was no escape; Muriel's Parisian

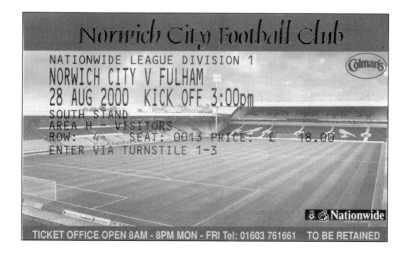

accent and haute couture won over Louis Saha while David Roodyn's fluent French and deep understanding of all things Fulham persuaded the manager of our honourable intentions.

At the Hotel Nelson in Norwich it was more entente cordiale than Trafalgar in August 2000. David Roodyn, exhibiting rather less haute couture than the fair Muriel, helped cement Anglo-French relations.

Come May 2002 most followers of the Fulham were in Cardiff with the Canaries, in spirit if not in person. Norwich City head to head with Birmingham City playing off for promotion to the Premiership. Bliss when the Canaries took the lead, gloom when they lost in extra time. I would have loved it, yes, I would really, really have loved it if this season's fixture card had included Norwich City. Instead we have Birmingham; farewell, fair Delia, bring on those Blues plus Paul Peschi's wife and Clinton's mum. As Ian Branfoot used to say: "It's time for hard hats and flak jackets."

Nottingham Forest

You spend years together in the second division. You expect to play them home and away. Thus it was in '72–'73 and '73–'74 but not in '74–'75. That was the year when we met them in league and cup. Six matches that season before Viv Busby settled it and we all staggered off to meet and beat the league leaders Everton.

Clough managed Forest then and he turned them from modest members of the second division into league champions, League Cup winners and over-lords of Europe (1979 and 1980).

Forest went up and up. We went down and down. I did not see inside the City Ground for many, many years (1975–2000). Come the French Revolution, Fulham and Forest met again on a sunny Saturday in September. The Clough era had transformed the City ground with the new Trent End and the Executive Stand. All very impressive and all the more comfortable for the Arundel/Haverhill contingent who were guests of the club, thanks to Chris the Physio.

Thus in a proper Premiership ground we awaited a first division fixture between the heirs of Clough and the young pretenders (P5, W5). No contest; Forest were awful and we were three goals up by half-time. The sun continued to shine, Forest continued to bumble and stumble, Fulham strolled about but to less purpose. Supporters stretched their legs—you can do that in the seats at Forest—spectators yawned and looked at their watches. Final whistle, three more points: P6, W6.

As I scuttled off to the station, I am sure I heard a familiar voice growling at the Trent: "Young man, young man—that was NOT very good."

Chris (the physio) Smith looked after old bones and old friends.

Notts County

County were very much part of our life in the 70s. Both County and Fulham had comfortable old stands with comfortable wooden seats and timbers beneath your feet. If and when it was a rousing contest, there would be much "Clap hands, stamp your feet, shout County/Fulham."

Rousing contests there were in the 70s with very few low-score bores. In '76 County thrashed us 5–1 at the Cottage. The very next September we thrashed them 5–1. In '76 John Mitchell was in goal, in '77 he went upfield and scored a hat-trick. Rousing contests in the late 80s with County winning 5–1 in '88 and Fulham storming away with the points in '89–'90. From 1–1 to 5–2 in a crazy second half at the Cottage. Goals from Milton, Mauge, Scott and Ivor sending us home happy.

Between these goal rushes County enjoyed their golden moment after 55 seasons away from the first division. With John Chiedozie on the wing they went at Forest and beat them home and away. Jimmy Sirrel took them up and Sergt. Wilko took them down. Come 1985 they were back in the third division ready to renew the entertaining struggle with Fulham. I remember Clive Walker waltzing the length of the field to score the goal of

Old Meadow Lane stand quite full; goalmouth very full—Fulham's visit in April 1979.

the season for ten man Fulham. An away win totally against the run of play. Almost as memorable for all the wrong reasons was a Harkouk frenzy up at Meadow Lane to match his frenzy at the Cottage when (in Palace colours) he attempted to strangle John Mitchell. They locked him away in the end— immensely talented but unreliable.

In September 1998 Fulham were unbeaten after six league matches, hence confidence as we approached Meadow Lane. Not the good old Meadow Lane of long ago but the Derek Pavis Stand. This "ninth wonder of the world" had been completed in 19 weeks for £3 million. (Fans had made off with the old timbers at £95 a yard.) Gone the wooden seats where Sheila's Uncle Harold Tooley had watched County win the fourth division title, gone the Trent Bridge stand where Lily Biggs had cheered for Jimmy Sirrel. Instead the "ninth wonder of the world" just as full of shiny new plastic as most of the modern stands we have visited from Chester's Deva to Scarborough's McCain Stadium.

Good view of the pitch and painful sight of Fulham missing six good chances while County made the most of their scoring opportunity. County 1 Fulham 0. Come the return match at the Cottage in February we had Geoff Horsfield to take those chances and we won 2–1. In addition we had Steve Finnan, acquired from Notts County in November for a modest fee and set to become "the ninth wonder of the World Cup" in July 2002. Fulham's Sean Farrell helped County win the third division title in '98; County's Finnan helped Fulham achieve 101 points in '99 and 2001.

Notts County have their brave new Meadow Lane; we have the Intertoto Cup and a place in the Premiership. But what wouldn't we give for those old wooden seats in those old wooden stands? "Clap hands, stamp feet…shout County/Fulham!" County 5 Fulham 1 in '76 and Fulham 5 County 1 in '77. Happy days, happy haze…or just distance lends enchantment?

Steve Finnan: number 6 for Notts County, September 1998; number 2 for Fulham, November 1998 to May 2003.

Notts County	V	Fulham
Darren **WARD**	1	Maik **TAYLOR**
Ian **HENDON**	2	Wayne **COLLINS**
Richard **LIBURD**	3	Rufus **BREVETT**
Matt **REDMILE**	4	Simon **MORGAN**
Chris **FAIRCLOUGH**	5	Chris **COLEMAN**
Steve **FINNAN**	6	Kit **SYMONS**
GARY **OWERS**	7	Peter **BEARDSLEY**
Andy **HUGHES**	8	Paul **BRACEWELL**
Sean **FARRELL**	9	Dirk **LEHMANN**
Gary **JONES**	10	Steve **HAYWARD**
Shaun **MURRAY**	11	John **SALAKO**
Chris **BILLY**	12	Gus **UHLENBEEK**
Alex **DYER**	13	Paul **PESCHISOLIDO**
MARK **QUAYLE**	14	Paul **MOODY**

On Safari

"**O**ut of Africa always something new," wrote Pliny 2,000 years ago. Out of Africa today—tremendous talent and a hunger for football and footballs. Hence the mission in 2001 of James Rettie (Harrodian School's FFC junior coach) to Nairobi; hence Harrodian visits to the street children of Cape Town in 2001 and 2002; hence the plans for links with township football in East London in 2003. All these initiatives involve FFC coaches, FFC sponsorship and invaluable help from FFC's Gary Mulcahey and Simon Morgan. Following the Fulham into Africa.

17th December 2001: Reconciliation Day in Cape Town and match day for Harrodians at the Homestead. 12 noon to Strand Street to meet up with Mr Headman (caretaker and referee). 12 noon = high noon = shoot-out, but not a penalty shoot-out. This was a real shoot-out between rival gangs with real bullets and real body bags. Fortunately the children were still up on Table Mountain so Mr Headman and I had three hours to sweep up after the police and ambulances had departed. Sweeping the pitch, removing broken bottles, tin cans and other dangerous objects; squatters remained encamped behind one goal but Mr Headman and I were just about ready to host the tournament at 3pm. The match went well for both teams and the final score 2–2 satisfied the Harrodians. Fulham and Palace shirts were presented to the Homestead and the great cake was devoured by players and supporters. Same again in December 2002—well, same presentation of Fulham kit and same feasting after the match but rather different weather and very different score: Homestead 5 Harrodians 2. That

"Friends of Fulham". Cape Town, December 2002.

Harrodian team had won all its fixtures in and around SW13, but it was beaten, and well beaten, in Cape Town.

In December 2001, while Sheila and I were taking Fulham into Cape Town, the James Rettie initiative in Nairobi was developing coaching and contacts. In December 2002, while Harrodians returned to the tournament on Muizenberg beach, James Rettie set out for Kenya with kit from Fulham and Palace, vowing to drive all the way in his Barnselona FC bus. However, he was frustrated by Egyptian officials and his precious cargo rests, even

"Footballs for Africa". James Rettie and his father in December 2002. Barnes to Budapest to Belgrade to Beirut—twelve countries in thirteen days.

now, in Jordan. In January 2003 James returned to London determined to accomplish his mission by other means: "This trip has only strengthened my thoughts about my goals for Africa."

South of Jordan but north of Cape Town another Fulham initiative has established links with township football. Juliet Slot and her husband met up with Bonnie, the headmistress of Qaqamba, East London, where there are many footballers but few facilities. Another good cause for Barnes and for FFC in 2003.

Then came the devastating news that James Rettie had been killed in a road accident. On 17th February 2003 St Michael's Church in Barnes was full, and mourners thronged churchyard, streets and Harrodian grounds in an attempt to honour an extraordinary enthusiast for football and for Africa. Gary Mulcahey and the Fulham community coaches gathered with Harrodian staff and Barnselona players to support the Rettie family and to confirm their backing for projects so precious to James: *Footballs for Africa*.

What is done and when it is done must await peace in the Gulf and the release of James Rettie's bus but somehow we will get the kit to Nairobi. Bonnie will get her football pitch and the Homestead will receive their tracksuits. Following the Fulham into Africa, bringing Africa back to Fulham. "This will be a successful project benefiting the people who need it most"— from James Rettie's diary for January 6th 2003.

In memoriam. James Pierre David Rettie (1974–2003).

Around the Grounds—Sailing

All aboard for the Orient—18th April 1992. From Craven Cottage to Greenwich Pier in an attempt to publicise Fulham 2000 and the fight to save the ground. Johnny Haynes, George Cohen and Jimmy Hill were on board for the second such sailing in September 1995.

Scenic and sociable, these river trips worked well as publicity stunts but showboats proved slow boats. Come Sunday 16th March 1997, and a mid morning fixture, and we were impatient—impatient for promotion and impatient with all those river bends and further delays at Greenwich Pier. So it had to be the Orient express and the Central Line: 19 stops, two goals, three points and back to Barnes in time for tea.

Cometh 2003 and Fulham 2000 has given place to BTCC. Back To Craven Cottage is organised by Fulham fan and GMB giant Tom Greatrex. By happy chance the final fixture was at Charlton, hence another opportunity to fight for Fulham while enjoying our riverside heritage. A bit of a natter about football with the founding father of the Fulham Academy, Alan Smith; a bit of a natter about Fulham with Sue Couch. Sue had helped to organise the trip to the Orient in April 1992. Eleven years on (one relegation and three promotions later) we are still agonising about Craven Cottage. Chin up; sunshine all the way and three points at The Valley—a grand day out and a stylish conclusion to a difficult season. Thank you, GMB and thank you, BTCC…plain sailing on 11th May 2003.

Seasoned campaigners: Sue Couch and Alan Smith.

Oxford

Accrington Stanley, proud aristocrats of the Football League, had become distressed gentlefolk by 1962. So distressed that they resigned in favour of Southern League champions Oxford United who under the captaincy of 'Big Ron' Atkinson made their way from the fourth to second division in double quick time. In 1968 Fulham failed to make their traditional late, late escape from relegation and met Oxford for the first time in September—Oxford 1 Fulham 0 at the Manor Ground—and in March 1969 Oxford completed the double with victory at the Cottage: Fulham 0 Oxford 1.

Following the Fulham to Oxford has been easier and jollier than travelling to Accrington Stanley. The M41/M40 links with Headington mean that you can drive from Hammersmith Bridge to the Manor ground in an hour/hour

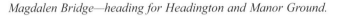

Magdalen Bridge—heading for Headington and Manor Ground.

and 10 mins. Better by far, however, is Park and Ride. Park just off the motorway and take the free bus into the city centre. Enjoy the stately prospect of the High, stroll through the cathedral close, walk from Christ Church to Magdalen Bridge; punting and picnics if the sun shines; Ashmoleum Museum and the Bodleian Library if it rains. As if the university itself was not attractive enough already Colin Dexter has now added the Morse heritage trail.

Lunch at Browns if it is too cold or too wet to picnic by the river, but it was perfect picnic weather in September '75 when we were still euphoric after our FA Cup adventures: "Oh, this year we're a going up, sing viva El Fulham!!" Whatever Oxford threw at us we returned with interest. Jimmy Conway's miskick rocketed off Johnny Mitchell's back and ended up in the Oxford net. Bobby Moore handled in the box but the referee had sun (stars?) in his eyes and waved play on. Viv Busby waltzed around the Oxford defenders and stroked the ball past keeper Milkins. All in glorious sunshine and we sang as we departed: "Oh, this year we ARE a going up!!" We didn't, of course, but we still look back on that game and those goals. (Walking from Hammersmith to Loftus Road for the WBA match this very February

Homely Manor Ground, homely fans.

- 77 -

the Busby goal at Oxford '75 was nominated for a place in our all time top ten.)

Lunch at Browns it had to be in March '81 and October '82. I was courting and did not want Sheila to catch cold before kick off. The sights had been seen, we had wined and dined. We were ready to walk across Magdalen Bridge and up the hill to Headington. Good for the digestion and the circulation, now to repeat the delights of September '75...Oxford 2 Fulham 0 in '81 and, as before, Oxford 2 Fulham 0 in '82. We returned for Wagner at the Playhouse, we returned for high table hospitality at The Queen's College, we returned for a graduation feast at Christ Church but we opted for Fulham 0 Oxford 1 in August '89 rather than Oxford 3 Fulham 5 at the Manor.

Oxford went on to higher things, much higher things: in 1986 they beat QPR 3–0 in the final of the League Cup. Oxford thrived on higher things in the old first division while Fulham were struggling in the third division. Indeed Oxford bought our best player. They took Ray Houghton for £150,000 with Jim Hicks as a bonus. What a blessing he proved! Jim Hicks soon became an icon at the Hammersmith End. Geoff Banton fans had to agree that their man might have to step aside. "Oh, lucky Jim, we remember him." Oxford graduate Jim Hicks as all-time Calamityman in defence?

In September 1993 Sheila and I returned to Oxford for a conference of headmasters. As I was due to retire that year my college kindly offered guest rooms. We enjoyed our stay apart from anxiety on the evening of 14th September. Fulham were in action but not at the Manor; no, our 'big game' was at Barnet. Wireless reports confirmed that Peter Baah had scored both goals and Fulham were fighting their way up the table. Baah scored again as we beat Barnet 3–0 at the Cottage but we did little else right that season and were relegated at the Vetch.

One of the very few regrets of recent years has been the lack of matches with Oxford. We celebrated promotion with a wonderful day out at Cambridge in May 1997 but we have missed out on the Manor 1989–2003. Indeed the Manor itself has gone. Heady days at Headington are just a distant memory but if you were there in September '75: "Oh yes, I remember it well..." Heady days and homely Headington with "Jimmy, Jimmy Conway, Jimmy Conway on the wing".

Peterborough

Peterborough has everything: fast trains from London, the Roman road, a medieval cathedral, modern shopping malls, an international rowing centre plus "the Posh". In April 1960 Fulham were celebrating 10th position in the first division with a 3–0 victory over the Arsenal. Peterborough's record was even more impressive: just one defeat in 103 matches 1957/58/59/60. The Posh took the fourth division title with ease in their first season in the league. Terry Bly scored 52 goals that year (and we thought Jezzard/Haynes/Ivor/Saha were prolific).

In 1965 as Fulham lost to Sheffield United in the first round of the FA Cup, Peterborough stormed into the sixth round with victories over QPR and the Arsenal. While Fulham were heading for the third division (1991–94), the Posh were enjoying life in the first division.

Fulham and Peterborough met three times in the League Cup in '75 and '76. October '75 at the Cottage was all Fulham but we lost 1–0. Much talk of the Alamo and bad luck but we lost and lost at home. The next August we avoided defeat at the Cottage thanks to a Les Barrett goal, and set off for Peterborough with George Best and Rodney Marsh. 16,476 spectators packed into London Road to watch the cabaret and the star of the show was— George Best with a goal from 30–40 yards. Followers of the Fulham still debate distance and distinction, but Best at Peterborough/Conroy at Wykham/

That Best goal. The Peterborough lights were not very bright, but Ken Coton managed to capture the ball on its way into goal from, well, 25 to 30 yards.

Harley at Loftus Road—take your pick, rewind your video, ask Ken Coton about the most golden goal.

Peterborough's London Road stadium sits just off the A1, hence its convenience for followers of the Fulham in general and the Thomsons in particular. Sheila and I can take in the match on our way to visit relatives in Lincolnshire. We were at London Road on 11th January 1992 when wind and rain meant cold comfort. Mud and blood from the Posh, mud and muck from the Fulham. A late penalty from Newson was the only cheering moment but cheer we did, even at 4–1 down. We danced and we chanted "Och aye, Don Mackay". Cheerful and full of cheer despite the miserable mismatch. Well done, those followers of the Fulham! On arrival in Lincolnshire there was precious little sympathy from Sheila's brother (sometime supporter of Forest) or Sheila's nephew (a passionate Chelsea fan).

For several seasons between 1992 and 1997 we drove up and down the A1 gazing with envy at Peterborough's ground and Peterborough's fixture list. If only we could be up in their division… Come 1997 and 1999 and 2001 it was Fulham up, up and up, while the Posh slipped down and down, despite the huff and puff of Barry Fry.

New Fulham are suddenly "posher" than Peterborough but London Road still has the edge on Loftus Road if you are looking for somewhere to park your car or stretch your legs.

Eating your Way Around the Grounds

Top ten grounds for pies and pints:
1. Value for money—Pride Park. The mushy peas were magnificent, piping hot and full of flavour. Especially good in the bitter cold of January 2002.
2. Vegetarian special—Carrow Road. Delia's own recipe at Delia's own diner. The waiter assured me that Delia had delivered the pies in person that very morning.
3. Fish and chips—Grimsby. To be enjoyed with a mug of strong tea. Do NOT ask for red wine at Blundell Park.

Fish and chips and ketchup down by the riverside—author and Sheila show the way.

4.   Red wine—Zagreb and Muizenberg. Great vintage wines at £2 a bottle.

5.   Cold collation—Ipswich. Salmon salad with Alf Ramsey, Bobby Robson and Richard Ryder. Generous host, distinguished photos, fine food…pity about the weather and Fulham's football.

6.   Hot soup—Hillsborough. Tomato soup and granary bread. Comfort food after difficulties by road and rail.

7.   Heinz tomato ketchup—always carry your own. Even the very best fish and chips (Grimsby and Scarborough) are imperilled by inferior ketchups.

8.   Mustard—take your pick. For Coleman's it has to be Norwich, but for the Dijon we recommend Sochaux.

9.   Pints with your pies—Newcastle. Blue Star Ales have fortified players and supporters for as long as I have followed the Fulham. Wor Jackie Milburn boasted that the FA Cup run of 1959 was powered by Newcastle brown ale.

10.   Cottage pie. Denis Compton wrote of all the goodies in the Cottage pie in November 1974 but catering at Fulham never really recovered from the resignation of Les Strong. Les captained us to promotion in 1981 before retiring to his pub in Richmond. The Clays loved their grub and Les Strong returned to the Cottage, but it all ended in tears, and our press-room tea ladies and our home-made scones were all that remained to delight the Good Food Guide inspectors in October 1994. (Two Hands publication: *A Record-breaking Journey through English Football* by Ken Ferris.)

Portsmouth

The Pompey chimes—"Play up, Pompey! Pompey, play up!"—a traditional chant, still going strong home and away. The Portsmouth chants and the Pompey chimes go back to the golden age of football when the fleet was in and when 50,000 watched Portsmouth play Derby at Fratton Park. The fleet was in then (February 1949) and the fleet had been loyal to Pompey since '39 when they beat Wolves to win the FA Cup. The fleet was at war and the league was suspended 1939–45 but with the return of the fleet and the revival of the league programme Portsmouth enjoyed crowds of 37,000 for several seasons. They won the championship in '49 and '50 with Jimmy Dickinson making 764 appearances between 1946 and 1965. By the time Dickinson retired Portsmouth were in decline. Just as Fulham always look to Haynes in a crisis so Pompey turn to Jimmy Dickinson. They made him manager and he took them out of the third division and into the fourth (1978).

Milan Mandaric has poured millions into rescuing the football but Fratton Park remains a bleak old ground. Visitors are seated but seated out in the open, not much fun as Pompey play up and the rain comes down. Thunder and lightning all morning in 2000 and dark clouds at 2.52 as Sheila and I took our seats. The Haverhill/Mortlake contingent were staying at Arundel with Roger, hence a relatively short retreat in the event of storms. Pompey had most of the play and deserved to win but a late free kick from Bjarne Goldbaek bobbled off their wall and into the net. Amazing—three points and it didn't rain. All smiles, we walked away through gridlocked traffic. One disgruntled motorist wound down his window: "Crap game, crap goal, crap team." We walked on as he remained fuming in the backstreets of Fratton.

Victory parade. Nelson's Victory *on the Friday, Fulham's victory on the Saturday. 12th February 2000, Portsmouth 0 Fulham 1.*

Pompey were still fuming in the backstreets when we returned on April 21st 2001. We were at the top of the table and Pompey were in the relegation zone. The fans were unhappy with manager Graham Rix and the chairman had just told Radio Solent that there was no more Mandaric money for new grounds or big name signings. Portsmouth had attempted to kick Fulham out of the game at the Cottage and had lost 3–1. The same tactics were adopted at Fratton Park and our new recruit Alain Goma was hurled off the pitch and into the moat. Insult was added to injury when Portsmouth took the lead and the chimes rang out. Old Fulham would have capitulated but Tigana's team were slick enough to dodge the worst of the challenges and regain the initiative through Boa Morte. In the 79th minute he was cut down in the box and Saha put away the penalty. 1–1 and we all went home happy.

Best of times at Fratton Park? 31st December '83: Portsmouth 1 Fulham 4 .Two goals from Ivor lifted us into the New Year. Worst of times at Fratton Park? September '80 when Fulham favourite Peter Mellor turned nasty and struck Ivor with a punch which went unseen by the referee. We lost 1–0 but that was not the end of the affair. I had driven little Mark and Brian Gee down to the match. Brian failed to reappear at 5pm. In a pre-mobile age one waited and waited, waited and wilted. Eventually Mark and I drove back to SW6 where anxious phone calls were answered with "What kept you?" Brian had failed to find us but had returned in style with a BBC TV film crew watching early versions of *Match of the Day*. Had Mellor's punch been recorded? I can't remember seeing it on air but I can still remember the incident and deep disappointment that one of our own from '75 should turn and rend us.

The great escape from Fratton Park? January 1985. Portsmouth go four goals up but Fulham fight back and at the very, very end Lock puts away the penalty for a 4–4 super draw. Perhaps an even greater result than Birmingham in August '79 where we were only three goals down at half-time.

With Harry the Red and his Bald Eagle in charge Pompey achieved promotion. Followers of the Fulham will soon be back at Fratton Park. Do we make a week-end of it? There is much to enjoy in the old dockyards. Nelson's *Victory*. Henry's *Marie Rose*, the ferry to the Isle of Wight. Cognoscenti visit an excellent Chinese restaurant at Arundel but there are plenty of fish to fry nearer the Solent. Many a site and merry the sight before you take your seat at the open end for a cacophonous chorus of Pompey chimes.

Sentimental Journey

Abenteuerroman. Sounds like East Germany's answer to the Leigh Railwaymen. Vielleicht Cottbus, Rostock RMI? No. Abenteuerroman includes three supporters from Hamburg but they are also Hammersmith

"Never mind the great heat…" July 2003, NOT February 1996.

Enders and followers of the Fulham. They joined a dream team of supporters, a team of supporters who dream. Abenteuerroman stands for followers of the Fulham on their sentimental journey.

July

In July they dream of promotion and cup runs as they assemble for the pre-season friendlies. Fixtures sponsored by Paul Kenny and GMB in Ballygar or by the lottery in Athens or by the Seagulls at Torquay. Never mind the great heat and the terrible T shirts, they travel in the hope of sighting a new signing or a youngster forcing his way into the senior team. They liked what they saw of Inamoto in Bologna… "Score in a moto, he's going to score in a moto." And he did. For once a new signing justified the hype by repeating the impossible in the final. Inamoto's hat-trick won a cup and UEFA status for Fulham. Inamoto's Intertoto of July 2002.

Youngsters pressing for places…remember that pre-season friendly between Fulham A and Fulham B back in July 1983? Johnny Marshall and Peter Scott dashing hither and thither at the Cottage while their elders and

John Marshall outpaces Alan Kennedy at Liverpool in November 1983.

once betters displayed their Majorcan tans to the ladies of Abenteuerroman. Come the start of the season Marshall and Scott were selected and the bronzed veterans were on the transfer list. In July 2003 Mark Hudson could not be faulted for work rate or skill at Plainmoor. Might he be one to watch as we turn to the Fulham Academy rather than France? The Abenteuerroman were cautiously optimistic on the slow train back to Paddington.

July is for dreaming and for deciding just which away fixtures are possible, which are probable and which are downright unmissable. Then Sky take their pick and the dates are changed so that the unmissable become the impossible.

August

The real thing again. 3pm, 18th August 1979—back to Birmingham and back to basics. Standing next to little Mark who is determined to do every match home and away. Solemn handshakes all round and never mind that Anglo-Scottish fiasco: Fulham 0 Birmingham 5. Within minutes we are three goals down but Fulham fan Keith Castle is pioneering heart transplants and some of his courage reaches through to the dressing-room. All change at half-time with three goals from Ivor and one from Guthrie. Birmingham 3 Fulham 4. Amazing!

Abenteuerroman indeed, even if it is down to earth and business as usual at the station with Birmingham supporters ambushing Fulham's stragglers and forcing them onto the railway track.

September

September's song is bitter sweet. Sweet enough at Griffin Park, 13th September 1980: Brentford 1 Fulham 3, but soon the bitter run of defeats culminating in Fulham 0 Oxford 4. Exit Bobby Campbell.

October

Golden October. Away to Millwall 17th October 1999 and an 89th-minute winner from Kit Symons. Up and down the Golden Mile, 31st October 1998,

Seasider Simon scores again. Golden October 1998. Blackpool 2 Fulham 3.

for goals from Morgan, Hayward and Horsfield—Blackpool 2 Fulham 3. Stand up if you're going up that golden October!

November

Fireworks in November. A firework display at Cleethorpes as Fulham beat Grimsby 4–0, 13th November 1982. More fireworks at Molineux with Fulham 3 Wolves 1, 20th November 1982. Those were the days… Both Chris and Dominic Guard followed the Fulham then. Ray Houghton ran the midfield and Ivor scored the goals.

December

Boxing Day blues in December 1977. We were all there. 55,000+ of us went to watch George Best kick a football and instead it was Micky Droy kicking George. A comprehensive kicking of Best with the inevitable red card for Best when he questioned the referee's eyesight. Chelsea 2 Fulham 0.

January, February, March

Bleak midwinter and few as bleak as 1951–52. Fulhamish to beat Middles-brough 6–0 and then free-fall for three months. Fulhamish to celebrate relegation with a 3–0 win over Derby. Bleak midwinter of 1951–52, my first season following the Fulham.

April

Spring fever in April 1980. Long before X3 XHM there was a rusty old, trusty old mini which took Abenteuerroman around the grounds. The map reader that April was the Oxford historian Julian Robins. He guided us through the back streets of Bristol to watch a Geoff Banton own goal gift the points to Rovers. Julian then directed us up to Vicarage Road on 19th April 1980 for Watford 4 Fulham 0: inept, fatal, relegation to the third division.

May

The merry month of May and very merry it was in 1997 as we celebrated our first promotion for 16 years at the Abbey Stadium (see chapter 28 *Following The Fulham*: Cambridge Carnival). More often, much more often, the month of May was both critical and painful.

In May 1983 Abenteuerroman gathered at the Baseball Ground for that crunch match/grudge match/match abandoned. Gathered in vain as Super Mac's team of all the talents failed to clinch promotion. Another May and another moment of madness—off went Moody in the first leg of the play-off against Grimsby at Craven Cottage, 9th May 1998; off went Pesch in the return leg up at Cleethorpes. Ten-man Fulham hanging on for 1–1 at the Cottage; ten man Fulham (superbly organised by Simon Morgan) hanging on for most of the away fixture. Final score, on aggregate, Grimsby 2 Fulham 1. Frustrated again but "NEXT May we're a going up!", and for once we jolly well were.

Abenteuerroman, being translated from the German, a sentimental journey, an entertainment with a serious purpose. Sentimental? Frequently. Entertaining? Yes—a weird and wonderful form of entertainment at times, but even in adversity the fellowship has made up for much of the misery.

Serious purpose? Very much so 1987–97. Serious and purposeful campaigning to save the club and the Cottage. Fulham 2000 had a serious purpose and a noble aim which is properly celebrated on the refurbished walls of the Stevenage Road stand.

June 2003 received from Tom Greatrex: "Thank you for joining the Fulham Supporters' Trust and becoming a member of the Back to the Cottage campaign..." What manner of memorial to BTCC? Back at the Cottage, August 2004. Now that really would delight Abenteuerroman and thousand upon thousand of followers of the Fulham. Away from South Africa Road and back to the Hammersmith End. "...sentimental journey home."

QPR

When Johnny Haynes and Ken Coton were creating Fulham's golden years there were two teams in West London: Fulham and Chelsea or, to be honest, Chelsea and Fulham. Come 1968–69 there was a change in the good old order as Fulham fell out of the first division and into the third. As we went down and down QPR were on the up and up: winners of the League Cup in 1967, promoted in 1967, promoted in 1968. Two teams in West London: QPR and Chelsea or, to be honest, Chelsea and QPR.

When my son took his place at the Hammersmith End in 1974 the new order was very much in place. Chelsea and QPR took the headlines, Fulham took the footnotes. True we went to Wembley in May '75 but the next May it was QPR almost taking the championship title while Fulham drifted from 3rd to 12th in the second division. QPR were competing in Europe, Fulham lost to Orient in the Anglo-Scottish Cup. Like it or not, QPR had overtaken us. I did not like it. The only enjoyable encounter with QPR in the 70s was an FA Cup match at the Cottage in January '79. Margerrison and Ivor scored for Fulham and we won 2–0. Stan Bowles danced about a bit and came out for the second half wearing gloves, commonplace now but much mock was made at the time.

Much more mock was made when QPR introduced their plastic pitch. Rangers had the last laugh in May '83. We were desperate for points to remain on course for promotion. We had the wrong footwear or the wrong mindset because we slithered and slipped all over their Omniturf. Ivor scored a late, late consolation goal but we were down and out 3–1 and down to ten men as Ray Lewington was sent off. Sent off, cheesed off and "cheated" by the artificial watering of an artificial surface to the obvious advantage of those who had regular use/abuse of such a pitch. Fulham were not the only moaners and groaners but by the time grass was restored to Loftus Road we were down in division three with Brentford.

QPR had not only overtaken us, they were ready to take us over. Fulham Park Rangers? The dream scheme in February 1987 (Marler masterplan) was for a merging of QPR and Fulham at Loftus Road. Leave Craven Cottage? Never! Fulham based at Loftus Road? Never!

Enter Jimmy Hill and the Muddymans to save Fulham. Johnny Haynes and many other former players pledged their support but not Paul Parker. From the lofty heights of Loftus Road the player we nurtured as a junior, as an apprentice, as a youngster in Super Mac's super team…this child of Craven Cottage suggested that a merger would do us good. "You know it makes sense!" Sensible possibly but totally unacceptable—better ten years in the wilderness than Loftus Road as our "promised land".

We endured our ten years (1987–1997) and we eventually returned from the wilderness as champions of the first division. Which team went down as we went up? QPR. Which team did we beat home and away for the first time in 70 years? QPR. Where do we celebrate survival in the Premiership? QPR. The unthinkable has been thought, the unacceptable in 1987 has been accepted for 2002. Accepted for 2002, accepted for 2003.

We all know why we went to Loftus Road. We had to move out for a season while Craven Cottage was superdromed for 28,000/30,000/40,000. We all suspected that such a stadium would take more than one season to

Must win, did win. Louis Saha opens the scoring at Loftus Road, 19th February 2003—Fulham 3 WBA 0.

complete. We all had reservations about Loftus Road as a home from home but at least it was still in the borough and, as Rufus Brevett assured us: "You can make a noise there."

Yes, we made a noise at Loftus Road when we beat Bologna and won that cup. Yes, we made a noise as we beat Bolton 4–1 to go top of the Premiership. Yes, we made a noise when came back from two goals down to beat Spurs 3–2. Yes, we made a noise when we beat Leeds and Liverpool and Newcastle. Yes, we made a noise when Barthez conned us: Fulham 1 Man Utd 1. Yes, we made a noise when Mr Winter turned up in Arsenal colours.

Oh dear, a sour note? A sore point? A touch tetchy? We ask questions in Bloemfontein Road and on Tunisia Terrace as we head towards the South Africa Road stand. Just what is going on? Out of Africa always something new? Out of Egypt always something new? "He wants to be a Brit and QPR are **it." Whatever QPR are, their home is Loftus Road. Whatever we were, our home was Craven Cottage. Whatever we are, our home is Craven Cottage. Whatever will be, will be; but will it be Craven Cottage?

Do we accept the advice of Paul Parker from 1987? Merge with QPR and live at Loftus Road? "You know it makes sense!"

Sensible did not save us in 1987 and sensible is not the answer in 2003.

County Grounds

Arnold, Ducat and Fender made 300 appearances for Fulham and between them scored 63 goals, but each the summer they left Craven Cottage for the Oval. Andy Ducat won England caps as a cricketer and as a footballer. The Compton brothers were formidable for Arsenal and for Middlesex but Highbury is not Lords. Craven Cottage is not The Oval. The county grounds are, or were, Northampton and Bramall Lane. Yorkshire cricket left Bramall Lane in 1974 and the Cobblers moved from the cricket ground to the Sixfields Stadium in 1994.

Followers of the Fulham have made many visits to Bramall Lane, and October 1977 was typical—elation and euphoria as Tony Gale scored, frustration and depression as Fulham faded and United won 2–1. Frustration and depression again in December 1985 and another 2–1 defeat. Frustration even for the champions in 2000–01 with 1–1 at Bramall Lane and 1–1 at Craven Cottage. The old Yorkshire cricket ground lacks the memories of Northampton where 24,532 watched Fulham in April 1966. Crowd record for the Cobblers and great escape for the Fulham. After four months at the bottom of the table Fulham won 4–2 at Northampton. Earle's hat-trick then was as entertaining as Mitchell's four against Orient in May 1977, but victory on the cricket ground meant another season in the first division. Mitchell saved us from the third division; Earle secured our seat at the top table.

David Pearce danced on the cricket field in April 1966 and he has followed the Fulham home and away for 40 years. Ken photographed him at Torquay in February 1996, disconsolate and gazing into the Conference. Sheila and I met up with him in Split in September 2002, well away from the Conference. Fulham in Europe.

In the good old days Northampton Town footballers were denied access to the cricket pavilion between May 1st and September 1st. Come September 2002 Fulham had already completed their Intertoto campaign plus three Premiership fixtures—eleven matches in the cricket season.

Taking the pitch at Northampton in April 1966.

Alan Ball—Wembley 1966 World Cup winner, Brockenhurst 1989 charity shield loser.

"The flannelled fools at the wicket…the muddied oafs at the goals." From 1888 to 1974 you could enjoy both at Bramall Lane and the County Ground, Northampton. Not any more; it's flannelled fools only at Northampton with muddied oafs confined to the Sixfield Stadium and Bramall Lane.

Wembley wizard and Hampshire Hog—Alan Ball in August 1989. Harry Redknapp's Bournemouth XI playing Alan Ball's Southampton XI at Brockenhurst. A friendly fixture which used to mark the end of the cricket season, just as the Cross Challenge at Walton used to prepare Hammersmith Enders for their return to Craven Cottage. Not this July, not this August; the Hammersmith End cricketers were in Finland, Greece, France, Italy and Croatia. Topsyturvydom rules as Surrey are at the County Ground, Northampton, in April playing cricket. From the Surrey County Cricket Club Journal for 12th April: "Who decided that the cricket season would start this early? Was it really necessary or sensible?" From the scorer at the County Ground at Northampton: "After four whole days in the pavilion at a very wet Lord's, it is good to get some cricket at Northampton…"

Topsyturvydom indeed—football in the heat of July and cricket in between April showers. The one month, too hot for football; the other month, too cold and wet for cricket. Time for Fulham fans and directors of Surrey (Micky Stewart and Victor Dodds) to talk some sense back into the seasons and while they're about it why not consider ground sharing at the Oval while the Cottage is revamped? Ample room on the terraces even on the day Surrey won the championship. Ample room for a football pitch or two without encroaching on the sacred square. The Oval has been used recently by Australians for their football tournaments and in years gone by for cup finals (FA Cup 1882: Old Etonians 1 Blackburn Rovers 0).

Ducat and Fender would beam down from J block if FFC were to join forces with Surrey.

Reading

Beer, bulbs and biscuits for years and years then part of the Maxwell empire and scheduled for Fulham Park Rangering via a shotgun marriage to Oxford. Exit Maxwell 1990, enter Madejski, thus Reading survive and prosper.

Not a local derby for Fulham but within easy reach by road or rail—part of that M4 corridor which seemed to dominate our season back in '81–'82. Up and down the M4 to Brentford, Oxford, Reading, Swindon, Bristol Rovers, Bristol City and Newport. We enjoyed the evening of 20th January 1982 after the big freeze and three weeks without football. (3–0 to Fulham with goals from Gale, Coney and Lewington.)

Another memorable encounter was the FA Cup match in November 1980. In addition to the usual fans, longing to repeat the cup run of '75, we had the enthusiastic support of the Fulham Rugby League team. A giant South African forward assumed that I was part of the FFC coaching team and told me to pass the word to Ivor and Tony Gale: "Liven up the action or we take over!" Fortunately the word sufficed—Ivor and Mahoney scored. We marched on

An R and an F on an old FFC Christmas card.

to beat Brentford and Bury before losing to Charlton while Fulham's rugby league team stormed to promotion.

Memorable for other reasons was a rain soaked thrashing 3–0 in October '92. Drenched and miserable, I was cautioned by the Reading police for inadequate cycle lights. I missed the fast train back to Richmond and got soaked again when the stopper dumped me back at Barnes.

The most extraordinary trip to Reading was May '89 when we were stumbling along in hope of a place in the play-offs. There was little to tempt followers of the Fulham to Elm Park—Super Mac season of '81–'82 it was not. On arrival at the visitors' end I was surprised to find not only the usual trio of Emanuel pupils but some dozen others lured there by James Norton's promise of goals, goals, goals. We did score eventually thanks to Justin Skinner but it was a drab match apart from the ferocity with which the Reading fans denounced their manager. "Branfoot out, Branfoot out", and out he was. He was on his way to Fulham via Southampton.

By the time followers of the Fulham had exhausted their own calls of "Branfoot Out" the Reading fans had a new ground, the Madejski Stadium. Bigger and better for sure but the playing surface suffers from ground sharing with rugby clubs. Our April 1999 visit found the pitch in poor shape and passing was difficult. Reading's star Mass Saar stumbled when through on goal and we survived various other scares before a Hayles cross was headed in by Simon Morgan. 1–0 to Fulham and I cycled off to the railway station confident of promotion.

Promotion followed eight days later as we beat Gillingham 3–0 and promotion took us away from Reading and the Madejski Stadium. Rugby matches continue to spoil their playing surface but Marcus Hahnemann seems equal to it all. Having been voted Nationwide player of the month for February 2003 he is enjoying tremendous success with the Royals. We may all meet again soon—preferably in the Premiership…

Simon Morgan heads the only goal of the game at Reading in April 1999. Reading fans' cries of "offside" seemed somewhat justified.

X Certificate

X as in X certificate; comes with a government health warning; not for those of a nervous disposition. Cold Blow Lane. Cold Blow Lane in December 1977 when Fulham went ahead 3–0 and the Millwall fans raced across the pitch to attack any and every visitor. The Baseball Ground. Derby in May 1983 when Hopkins and Wilson were assaulted and the match was abandoned. The winter of our discontent 1986–87 with Craven Cottage sold and FFC packaged up as a subsidiary of QPR. Relegation to the third/fourth division in May 1994. Humiliation at Lincoln, Mansfield and Torquay in midwinter 1996. And 91st place in the league. All in all X certificate; not for those of a nervous disposition.

That was Old Fulham. New Fulham do not go in for X certificates. New Fulham is all about titles, medals, trophies and the Premiership. Eventually, yes; but have you forgotten some of those 0–0s served up by Ray Wilkins? Then bracing yourself for a lot more of the same under PB? Perhaps not X certificate, but certainly XB for extra boring.

Fulham v Leicester in May 2002 should have been Tigana v Adams and the best of New Fulham welcoming back the saviour of Old Fulham but it descended into bathos and worse as we realised that we were leaving the Cottage not with a bang but with a yawnsome whimper 0–0.

Loftus Road has well documented X certificate features, but at least it is only for a year or two while the superdome/superdrome is under construction. Pause for black clouds over that golden prospect in February 2003 as suddenly we hear that Craven Cottage has been sold? Put on hold? Questions are asked and the press ruin breakfasts for a month or three with insider stories of insider dealings plus mounting uncertainty about Tigana and his contract. More than a hint of X certificate here?

Time out for the FA Cup replay at Turf Moor—just what we need to restore morale and right the wrongs of 50 years. X certificate first half followed by double-X second half with a red card for Sean Davis and humiliation (yet again) at the hands/feet of Burnley.

And so into the crunch month without our player of the season…high noon at Old Trafford: Van N 3 Fulham 0. Never mind, Blackburn at Loftus Road must offer a chance to turn things around. If we were bad at Turf Moor, we were worse on 7th April 2003. "Things fall apart; the centre cannot hold,

the best lack all conviction." Fulham 0 Blackburn 4—and it could have been more—plus all on Sky for the world to note our plight. Groundless, manager-less and clueless. W. B. Yeats encapsulated our predicament: "Mere anarchy ... things fall apart." Truly X certificate on and off the pitch with JS the Undertaker muttering in the press box and Dave Gardner grumbling to the vice presidents. "Team in disarray, club in disarray." Those very words overheard twice within five minutes of the final whistle.

As the guest of Bill Muddyman that evening I had the opportunity to talk matters over with the vice chairman and Paul Kenny of GMB. Somehow the conversation turned to Ashford and an earlier crisis. Two goals down and sinking under the flood waters…floundering about until Micky Adams came to our rescue.

Cycling home later, much later, I refused to return the various calls on the answer machine. Cometh the dawn, cometh the dawn chorus of messages comparing the Blackburn match with Fulham 0 Oxford 4 in October 1980. Campbell out, Tigana out.

Look to the rock.—Isaiah, chapter 51, verse 1. Having put my suggestions on the boardroom table after the debacle of 7th April, it was a matter of watching and waiting and trusting in the Muddymans. The Muddymans have been our rock 1987–2003.

Five days on and we are off to Anfield for Liverpool 2 Fulham 0. Next up Newcastle pressing for the Champions League while we are changing managers and longing for something to cheer—and cheer we did for Chris Coleman. On my way into Loftus Road on that Saturday, 19th April, I bumped into Simon Morgan. Confident and confidential came the whispered words: "Watch the difference…" Watch the difference indeed. *Vive la difference* at Stamford Bridge on the 26th of April. We looked to the rock, we looked within for salvation, we looked for guts, we found the feelgood factor. "Happy days are here again?"

May 11th and off to Charlton where we saw all the old flicks and tricks from 2001. Another away win, 48 points and safe for another season. Congratulations and thank you, Chris Coleman!

No longer managerless, no longer clueless, panic over and X certificate lifted. With Fulham, however, the X-certificate is like the sword of Damocles: lifted but still hovering just above our heads. Hovering, looming, threatening until we regain our own ground.

Walking Around the Grounds

Football Fanatic by Ken Ferris demonstrates how to visit all 92 grounds in a single season. No doubt the *Guinness Book of Records* lists other fanatics who have walked their way around all those grounds. Followers of the Fulham have their very own pedometers: Alex Ferguson and Captain Beaky Billing (pictured), who walked from Craven Cottage to the Goldstone in aid of Fulham 2000. When Captain Beaky set sail for the Orient in April 1992 others walked from the Cottage to Brisbane Road (Dom and Will Guard).

We have all walked from Craven Cottage to Stamford Bridge or from the Bridge to the Cottage (some thousand did so this very April). Craven Cottage to Griffin Park is a very pleasant stroll along the towpath. With what glee I recall the way Peter Beardsley picked Brentford pockets in April 1998 to set up both Moody's goals! Craven Cottage to Loftus Road is a less agreeable walk—home sweet home to home from home via the Bush and White City traffic fumes. Never mind, it is much quicker on foot than by car or bus.

Walking the Wembley Way? We did it once. The going was easy but the return was less than jolly.

Jollier than jolly and better than good was the walk from Craven Cottage to Barnes Bridge on the evening of 21st April 1999. Oh yes, you remember it well—Fulham 4 Millwall 1. Clinching the championship at the Cottage and doing so by totally outplaying traditionally difficult/bruising/intimidating opponents and silencing their formidably vocal supporters...oh yes, we remember it well. Son-in-law Piers and I walked the walk, talked the talk, danced the dance, even floated the float and (forgive us) gloated the gloat. Somewhere beyond Putney Bridge the common was on fire. Oh woe; had Millwall resorted to arson? No, 'twas but the flames of tarmacadamers resurfacing Rocks Lane. A grand glow at midnight as we grinned our way past Barnes Pond. And so to bed as champions, our first title for 50 years. Well worth the walk.

Sheffield Wednesday

Scunthorpe, Sheffield United, Sheffield Wednesday, Shrewsbury, Southampton, Southend, Southport, South Shields, Stockport, Stoke, Sunderland, Swansea and Swindon and, more recently, Scarborough and Split: S is easier than J. Scarborough has much to offer (sea, sand, history and theatre) but with over 100 fixtures in the Fulham archive the Sheffield clubs demand attention.

Followers of the Fulham know both grounds well but Hillsborough means more to us than Bramall Lane because of April 5th 1975. Fulham were up at Hillsborough for the FA Cup semi-final with Birmingham. Hillsborough was where Johnny Mitchell became Super Mitch with the most spectacular goal of his career which inspired the most spectacular of Ken Coton's many Fulham photographs. Look at the front cover of *Fulham's Golden Years* and roll back the years.

John Mitchell begins his celebration run in April 1975.

Forward to 1989 and Hillsborough assumes a very different meaning. Heysel and Hillsborough hit Liverpool hardest but the consequences of the Taylor report meant major changes at many grounds. Indeed the implications of the Taylor report for Craven Cottage are probably painful and possibly terminal.

In happier times Fulham have prospered at Hillsborough. In December 1973 we won 3–0 with goals from John Conway—yes John Conway—Barrett and Busby. My photograph is from a game in October 2000 that we almost lost. Torrential rain and a heavy pitch did not suit Tigana's team who were a goal down at half-time. Those photographed were muttering about Fabrice Fernandes who clearly didn't relish Yorkshire in bleak midwinter. Barry

Wednesday 3 Fulham 3 in October 2000. A bit of a result and a sort of a smile.

Hayles must have heard because he bustled us back into the game. Bazzzzzzzzah! We took the lead (twice) but Wednesday equalised (twice). Given the conditions 3-3 was a fair result and some of those photographed managed to smile.

Good as we were in that season of seasons we couldn't beat United or Wednesday in Sheffield and we couldn't beat United or Wednesday at the Cottage but we could smile on Monday 16th April 2001. We could grin from ear to ear and here to there because that Sean Davis goal clinched the first division title: Championeeeeeeeeeeeze! Same faithful followers of the Fulham—very different expressions at the final whistle.

Lost Grounds

Accrington Stanley—a beautiful name from the beautiful game. Onomatopoetic. Accrington Stanley—northern grit and grime. Once proud aristocrats of league and FA Cup, Accrington Stanley fell upon their swords in the 60s. Followers of the Fulham went to Gainsborough Trinity and Glossop North End in the league, they went to Leigh Railwaymen's Institute in the FA Cup, but the nearest they got to Accrington Stanley was Alf Toothill (Alf the Birdcatcher was a cricketer from Ramsbottom who made 203 appearances in goal for Fulham).

Accrington Stanley were going when the going was good and Fulham were established escapologists at the foot of the first division. When Fulham finally fell and fell through the second division into the third (1969–70) they might have expected to meet Accrington Stanley along with Barrow, Halifax and Rochdale. Too late. Accrington Stanley had lost their league status to Oxford.

"Accrington Stanley are going, are going, are going, are gone." Many others followed. Some bounced back: Lincoln and Doncaster. Others may yet return: Shrewsbury and Exeter? Many old friends remain in the wilderness: Aldershot where we lost on penalties 10–1 in February 1987; Chester where we lost 7–0 in April 1989; Halifax where Steve Earle scored five goals in the 8–0 victory of 1969; Maidstone where we won 6–2 in October 1991; Newport with the rusty roof and terrible tea where we won 3–1 in the promotion push of March 1982; Scarborough with its cricket festival, castle, Ayckbourn theatre and Rob Scott.

Barrow, Gainsborough, Glossop North End, Merthyr, Nelson, Southport, South Shields and Thames Association are all grounds graced by FFC and enjoyed by followers of the Fulham. In 2003 you may know little and care less about Glossop North End…but Wimbledon? Wimbledon—winners of the FA Cup and a Premiership club for more years than Fulham. Followers of Wimbledon have a remarkable tale to tell but with relegation came crisis and disenchantment, division and receivership. Wimbledon renamed, Wimbledon reshamed…the lessons from Accrington Stanley mean little to us today but the lessons from Wimbledon are there for followers of the Fulham to read, mark, learn and inwardly digest. Without Plough Lane the club was at risk. Ground sharing on unequal terms was unpopular and unprofitable. The Milton Keynes solution was not acceptable to the fans and thus became unworkable.

Loss of ground equated to loss of home which equalled loss of heart which resulted in loss of life.

Yesterday Accrington Stanley, today Plough Lane. Tomorrow Craven Cottage? Expensive and dangerous days for football clubs. Especially dangerous for the groundless and homeless clubs of South West London.

Showgrounds

The greatest of the showgrounds is at Peterborough—not merely county shows but regional, national and international events. Showjumpers gathered at Peterborough in 1985 and 1991 and my grandchildren from Derby opted to watch the horses rather than the football.

Grandsons who prefer the pony club to the Posh.

The delights of Peterborough United and their London Road stadium are discussed elsewhere (page 79). The second best showground is at Hereford with its cattle market and cider mills—please see Hereford chapter. There used to be a mighty showground at Boston where the market tolls and harbour dues were second only to those of the City of London (as revealed in the

Pipe Roll audit for July 1203 to November 1204). Boston, however, is not yet a Fulham ground so let us hasten off to Shrewsbury.

Shrewsbury has showground, markets and coracles. Indeed Shrewsbury Town is the only football club to retain a coracle man on the groundstaff. Fred Davies was supposed to retire at 86 but his son could not control the coracle so Fred had to return to duty as matchday ball boy. Followers of the Fulham are comfortable at Shrewsbury where the Gay Meadow stadium reminds them of Craven Cottage—beside the waters of the Severn and boasting a Riverside Stand.

Early in the season of 1982–83 we drifted down river to the RSBC boathouses as guests of loyal 'Shrew' Dominic

Shrewsbury, another riverside ground with another riverside stand.

Willsdon. September 4th was warm work for spectators and almost impossibly hot for both teams. Exhaustion, dehydration and torpor seemed to have resulted in a drowsy draw 0–0. ("Let's get back to the riverside watering holes.") Suddenly Robert Wilson woke the Fulham faithful with a solo run and a mighty strike—Viv Busby at his best could not have improved on that solo run and Clive Walker would have been pleased with the power of that shot. Game over and Dominic devoted his evening to artwork in honour of the Fulham fans. The original was presented to Malcolm Macdonald who, as always, wrote promptly and warmly in reply.

Come October 1984 we returned to the Gay Meadow but Robert Wilson was not selected and the score remained 0–0. We lost in January 1985 but it did not harm our middle of the table team (9th in November and December, 9th in February, April and May). Marshall and Pike scored at the Cottage in October 1985 as we muddled our way to 16th place, but March 8th away to Shrewsbury was critical with Fulham in 21st place and floundering. Sheila and I bumped into Jim Stannard and Ray Harford at the *Lion* in Shrewsbury. Jim was cheerful enough but the manager looked anxious; the hotel required two FFC directors to sign the cheque for lunch and in those difficult days there weren't any directors willing to follow the Fulham to showgrounds such as Shrewsbury. Sympathetic words from simple fans must have meant something to Ray Harford because he thrust directors box tickets upon us and promised goals as soon as Chris Pike returned to lead the line. No Pike that day and it was left to Gary Barnett to provide a late consolation goal— but all in vain, all in vain, for FFC had lost again. We were relegated and for several seasons looked up with envy at the mighty Shrews.

Oh dear, how we struggled to contain them in an FA Cup tie at the Cottage in January 1996. Terry Angus scored to make it 1–1 and send us back to Shrewsbury where the winning team would cash in on Liverpool as third round opponents. Fulham went ahead through Rory Hamill and Shrewsbury were down to ten men. *Ten men went to mow, went to mow Gay Meadow*— and those were the days when Fulham always lost to ten men. Even the lure of Liverpool could not lift our eleven who succumbed 2–1. Gloom, all pervading gloom—we were desperate for success and desperate for the money. Robert Wilson's super goal and Macdonald's super management, those were the days long, long ago and far, far away.

Ray Harford (1945–2003) masterminded Fulham's promotion in 1982.

Hooray for the FA Cup: January 2003 with third division Shrewsbury beating Premiership Everton. Gay indeed was the Meadow. Showboating on the showground and a carnival of coracles down by the riverside.

Three months on and the two prettiest football grounds in the English league are at risk. Craven Cottage closed and Gay Meadow relegated to the Conference. Fulham supporters know what it is like to be 91st in the table. Our sympathy is with the Shrews as they suffer down by the riverside.

In April 2003 as I searched for photos of the coracleman there were many conversations with the Sandras and Yvonnes of Shrewsbury Town. Courteous and constructive, they put me in touch with their Dennis Turners and their Ken Cotons. Again and again my questions were answered; again and again there were friendly references to former fixtures. They admire our

Thames while we enjoy their Severn. Stuart Dunn of the *Shrewsbury Chronicle* was especially helpful and very well informed on FFC.

What a contrast with officialdom at Stamford Bridge where I requested a photo of Peter Bonetti. Juniors had never heard of him and more senior officials called the Cat 'old hat' and of no interest to New Chelsea. Frustrated I mentioned all this to our very own Mark Maunders who supplied me with a top quality transparency within the hour. Thank you, Mark, and thank you, Stuart! Fulham and Shrewsbury will never be as trendy as Chelsea but at least we retain civilised manners while avoiding vainglorious strutting and arrogance. Lovers of *The Wind in the Willows* will know what I mean: Fulham and Shrewsbury are Mole and Ratty (humble riversiders); as for Chelsea…very much Toad of Toad Hall.

Around the Grounds by Car

Car free and carefree, I followed the Fulham for 30 years (1951–1981) not knowing what I was missing. Come the promotion season of '81–'82 it was car full and careful; car full to help with the petrol, careful because of the great freeze. We seemed to spend an inordinate amount of time slithering up and down the M4: the oft postponed game at Hereford, Bristol Rovers away in cup and league, Bristol City away, Swindon away, Reading away, plus, at the very far end of the M4, Newport. My map reader put me into a snow drift on the way to Swindon but we lifted the mini back onto the road and reached the County Ground in time for goals from Ivor, Ivor, Lock and O'Driscoll.

The next season I exchanged two back-seat drivers (male) for a co-driver (female). Courtship and marriage improved car journeys around the grounds. We started on September 4th at Shrewsbury and continued via Grimsby and Cambridge to Derby on May 14th. The next season it was Shrewsbury, Cambridge, Brighton, Swansea and Derby. Romance on the road and romance off the road with long walks on the Mumbles shore and visits to the home of Dylan Thomas.

In football (as in art, music, diet and dress) my wife taught me to be more selective. Following the Fulham around the grounds we have striven for quality rather than quantity. That is where the car proves its value: Mary Doughty's coach and Chris Topley's train have to rush there and back on match days, but with the car comes the chance to go early or return late. Cambridge by car means time in the university bookshops as well as two hours at the Abbey Stadium. Derby by car involves visiting the grandchildren for solace after the Baseball Ground. Grimsby is Kirton Skeldyke and Skegness in addition to Grimsby 0 Fulham 4.

Long gone is the mini to be replaced by Sheila's Fiat (favourite ground Gay Meadow with its riverside setting and the coracle man as ball boy). In May 1993 it was off to Chester by Peugeot for two goals from Brazil and the winner from Captain Morgan. The '97, '99 and '01 promotion years have been in X3 XHM—an extraordinarily generous retirement present from a former pupil.

We longed for the Premiership after 33 years in the lower leagues, but having arrived what have we gained as away day grounds? Vast stadium after vast stadium but few of them have the character and atmosphere of yesteryear's Gay Meadow, Goldstone, Edgar Street, Bootham Crescent, Vetch Field. Sheila has certainly enjoyed Intertoto and EUFA travel but her visits to Bologna, Split and Zagreb were not by car and she has not been tempted into X3 XHM for Aston Villa, Birmingham or West Bromwich. Sufficient unto the train are the evils thereof. The romance of the road, like Craven Cottage, is a sweet but distant memory.

"Those were the days…" Right car, right results—P11 W11, October 2000.

Sochaux

A remote corner of France but home to the Peugeot works team—Sochaux and our destination on 7th August 2002. The first leg had provided an introduction to life at Loftus Road plus a belated but well constructed goal fashioned by Inamoto finished by Davis.

Sean Davis, born Battersea September 1979. Davis made his first appearance for Fulham in October 1996; five years and four divisions later he was playing for us in the Premiership. Six years on Davis was central to our Intertoto campaign. This Battersea Rise headmaster was determined to follow the Battersea boy into Europe.

Others were Buzzing it from Stanstead to Dijon but I opted for Eurostar via Ashford—yet more nostalgia there. The Paris leg was easy and the train to Dijon was comfortable. The final section to Sochaux tested my knowledge of French routes and time-tables. If only Steven or Andy had been there to calm me… Enfin, enfin after 12 hours of express plus local stopper, starter, stopper I was there with 20 minutes to spare for a brisk trot to the ground.

A neat and tidy stadium decorated in Peugeot blue and gold. Peugeot lions on the banners and Sochaux tigers on the pitch. Benoit Pedretti was too

tigerish for Herr Wack and was dismissed. Truly excellent goals from the head of Legwinski and the boot of Hayles gave Fulham victory. 2–0 on the night and 3–0 on aggregate.

Job done and just one minor matter to settle before heading home: accommodation? Mercifully the bonny boys had booked a hotel in Dijon. The slow train from Sochaux got us to bed before breakfast and the early morning sunshine warmed our way to the medieval cathedral. Plainsong in the choir, a bishop addressing the faithful, sunlight on ancient stone and somewhere at the back of my mind a link between these Dijon ceremonials and the people of Glastonbury. Twelve hours later in Mortlake I could check the Anglo-Saxon Chronicle for 1083. Abbot Thurstan had forced Dijon chants upon the choristers. The local folk insisted on singing the old familiar words to the old familiar tunes. Bloodshed ensued with Frenchmen invading the choir and three Anglo-Saxon monks "done to death and eighteen good people wounded."

Followers of the Fulham have their old familiar words and their old familiar tunes. Our song for Sochaux, our Dijon chant for 2002? "You all support Switzerland, you all support Switzerland!" Such topographical taunts proved of little interest to the well armed gendarmerie who yawned their way through our Anglo-Saxon anthems. We returned unbloodied and unbowed. "Sochaux vaut bien une messe."

Grounds We Hate

Burnley, of course, because we never win there and Birmingham because there is always trouble. In my 52 years on the road with FFC we have never won at Burnley and the natives are far from friendly. We have won at St Andrew's: in August 1979 we were three goals down at half-time but won 4–3 and in August 2000 we won in style 3–1, but before, during and after the match there was trouble from the Birmingham fans. Bottles, bricks and broken windows in 1979; coaches wrecked in 1999 and 2000.

Millwall? My son and I had trouble at Cold Blow Lane in December 1977 (pitch invasion when Fulham won 3–0). There were, also, anxious moments at Elland Road in April 1983 when stewards let the Leeds fans into the Fulham end.

But Burnley and Birmingham remain the grounds to be avoided.

I took against Turf Moor back in 1952 after a couple of unfortunate experiences with Burnley supporters, and I have not returned to those parts.

My intrepid colleague Derek has persevered despite our terrible record there. As champions in 1999 we might have hoped for something but Morgan, Betsy, Horsfield and Pesch were roughed up and to their injuries were added the usual insults plus, on this occasion, a bizarre red card for Kit Symons. An unhappy end to an unhappy afternoon.

If that was bad, the FA Cup game in 2003 was worse. Relegated Grimsby managed to put six goals past Burnley, relegated Wednesday won 7–2 at Turf Moor, but Premiership Fulham never looked like scoring. We started badly, got worse, and lost Sean Davis at a crucial stage of the season. It all made for miserable viewing on TV, but Derek insisted on attending in person and filed the following match report plus a considered conclusion to his 35 years at Turf Moor.

The Turf Moor Two—Derek and Steve cheerful in adversity, February 2003.

Burnley could be described as a quaint old-fashioned backwater, but a more accurate description would be the land that time forgot. It is an insular place, where visitors are always given a 'warm' welcome, both on and off the pitch.

My first game there was during the 1976–77 season. Fulham took the lead through Les Barrett, but it was downhill after that. Burnley ran out 3–1 winners, and Fulham continued their run of not having won at Turf Moor since 1951. As most fans know, the run continues to this day. Since then I have seen nearly all of the Whites' games at the Moor, and it is particularly irritating that I missed the draw of October 1981, a rare success!

I don't have many pleasant memories of Burnley, and unfortunately foremost amongst the unpleasant ones is the racist abuse that Rufus Brevett received in 1997–98. Anti-racism campaigns had yet to reach this part of West Lancashire. It came as no surprise that the BNP targeted the area and currently holds eight places on the Burnley Borough Council.

I shall always remember the way that Rufus dealt with the abuse. He just got on with the game. We all remember Rufus fondly, because he was the model professional, who gave one hundred per cent and genuinely cared for the club and the fans.

Split

Croatia's bloody history tells of war after war and atrocity after atrocity on the long, long road to freedom. Croat struggles began back in 855 and paused a thousand years on in 1995. Terrible loss of land and life in 1991 (10,000 dead) was revenged in 1995 with the rape, torture and massacre of Serbs at Knin. Two Croatian generals remain on trial charged with war crimes.

What has all this to do with Fulham and football? Everything. The front page of the local paper placed the generals alongside the Hajduk match report. The banner above both stories is BEZ NADA. Bez nada—without hope the generals defy the international courts, and bez nada—without hope the Hajduk Split team travel to London. Be warned, however, because their patron, Goran, was unseeded and without hope when he travelled to London in 2001. Wounded and without hope, he was 6–0 down to Henman in the semi-final. Wounded and without hope, he won Wimbledon. Wounded and without hope, Goran will lead them out at Loftus Road. Be warned and be ready.

Bez Nada is the clue to 'Torcida' and the fanatic supporters of Hajduk Split. Remember those international matches when the Croatian team contained ten players from Hajduk Split and just one "foreigner' from Dinamo Zagreb. Remember that the symbol of their support is the flaming torch and remember that the home end features a memorial to the Torcida martyrs from 1991–95. "Football is not a matter of life and death—it is much more important than that." For the followers of Hajduk Split football is indeed a matter of life and death with the sum greater than the parts. Take the banners on Thursday night: "William Wallace" because the bravehearted Scot defied the English overlords. Take the club mascots on the T-shirts: a braying jackass trampling on the British bulldog. Smirking Dalmatians mounting English hounds. Such artwork prepared Croatians for the humiliation of FFC on 19th November 2002. These garments were on sale throughout town and when I left Split on the 21st the market traders boasted that their entire stock had sold out despite the match result.

Head waiter Zlatco declares that Roy Keane is a true Torcida. Torcida of Torcida because he despises his English overlords. The abrasive Irishman (Keane) and the abrasive Scot (Sir Alex) are honorary Croatians. IRA and Tamil Tiger slogans are daubed all over the walls. Violence and racism are part and parcel of team and town. "No one likes us, we don't care" and there is much of Millwall about Hajduk Split. Take the old Millwall ground at Cold Blow Lane and the National Front vitriol directed at black players—same again in Split. Remember those pitch invasions of the 1970s when teams took the lead against Millwall. December '77: Millwall 0 Fulham 3 with their fans on the pitch, hurling seats at followers of the Fulham.

The Torcida can't throw seats because there aren't any but insults and fireworks are directed at opponents. The fire brigade are busier than the stewards as the sun goes down and the rockets go up. Explosions, smoke, dust and flames make Torcida happy and visitors anxious. Tigana who experienced defeat here with Bordeaux (1–4) prepared Fulham for the ordeal by fire with video footage of Hajduk in flames.

My wife loved Bologna where followers of the Fulham were applauded all the way back to cathedral square. She was much less comfortable in Split despite the police escort and dog patrols. Mean streets and menacing tower blocks; no singing, no dancing. Clinging on to that away goal, we took sanctuary in the hotel Globo. Sad to say but the hatred followed us off the streets and into the hotel. The night porter (pictured right) was just back from the match and berated Fulham as Imperialist agents of Anglo/Yugoslav militarism. I pointed out that when the Croatians were fighting for freedom in 1995 we were struggling for survival at the wrong end of the third division. He retorted with references to Harrods. Our chairman was depicted as a Moslem mafiaman threatening Catholic Croatia. Slobadan the porter then turned our Al Fayed chants against us. Why does he want to be a Brit? Because he wishes to join the corrupt oligarchy twisting international politics to the detriment of small independent nations such as Croatia.

Eventually I opened my passport at place of birth: EDINBURGH. Suddenly all was forgiven. I was a 'victim', bez nada, and thus honorary Torcida. Come the dawn and William Wallace was not the only Scot to merit a banner in Split.

What to Wear Around the Grounds

Fashionable Fulham? The Pope and Charlie Chaplin, Honor Blackman and Angie Best, Hugh Grant and Nasty Nick, Michael Jackson and his parasol…fashionable, certainly, but few of them follow the Fulham around the grounds. Hence this selection of garments modelled by the chairman and supporters. Please note the Fulhamish delight in hats and caps rather than replica shirts.

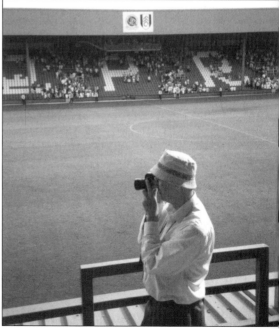

Torquay

Better than Brighton? Nicer than Nice? Trendier than St Tropez? Certainly the Famous Four enjoyed their big day out at Torquay in September 1991. Express train following the South Devon coastline, sunshine, swimming, beach football and picnic. Taxi to Plainmoor in ample time for meeting and

greeting with players and fans. Big Jim Stannard keeping Fulham in the game, Udo Unwere heading us into the lead and a rare away win.

Such were the delights of Torquay that it seemed just right for a half-term holiday in October 1992. Fulham were due to play at Exeter so Sheila and I revisited Torquay, enjoying late autumn sunshine and exploring the Teignmouth–Dawlish coastline. The early bus into Exeter on the Saturday and a look around the cathedral before our first experience of Grecian fare. St James Park had old fashioned wooden stands which went well with the old fashioned tones of the MC. He reminded me of John Snagge on Boat Race day and he proved as articulate as David Hamilton. The match itself was dominated by Julian Hails who set up two goals for Sean Farrell. The second half contained many scares for followers of the Fulham: scares generated by eccentric refereeing, scares generated by eccentric passing.

I can't remember the name of the referee but most of the wayward passes were from the boot of KJL. Karl Junior Lewis went on to much higher things and even graced the Premiership with Leicester but that October day was not his day. Fulham fans urged Don Mackay to replace Junior with Tierling. Such questioning of Junior's skills brought forth the inevitable retort: "You think Junior Lewis is bad, you should have seen Senior Lewis—now he really was poor..."

Somehow Fulham managed to hang on for a 2–1 win and we celebrated with scones and Devon cream before catching the bus back to Torquay. "Better than Brighton, nicer than Nice and trendier than St Tropez?" Well, in late October St Tropez is empty but Torquay buzzes with cookery courses at the Imperial Hotel and wine tasting at the Grand. Thus we all agree that Torquay is THE place for holidays but there have been too many, far too many disappointments on the pitch: September '94, February '96, January '97, January '99; four visits to Plainmoor; four defeats. The most alarming result of all was Torquay 2 Fulham 1 in '96. This left us in 91st place and

February 1996—nadir and nightmare.

provoked scenes in the car park. Arundel Roger demanded answers of Bill Muddyman. "Branfoot out and Adams in." Enter Micky Adams but even his promotion team were beaten home and away by Torquay. Enter Kevin Keegan but even his championship winners lost their cup game at Torquay.

Behold a paradox: Torquay, that jewel in the crown of South Devon; Plainmoor, that thorn in the flesh of Fulham. Solution—go there in June and watch the cricket but leave Plainmoor to the gulls and the Gulls.

J Block

*R*obert Frederick Charles Moore: 12th April 1941–24th February 1993. David Hamilton greets followers of Fulham and Sunderland at Loftus Road and reminds us that it is the 10th anniversary of the death of Bobby Moore. What has all this to do with FFC in 2003? Nothing if you are Hammers because Bobby Moore belongs to Upton Park but everything if you were at Wembley in '75. Alec Stock brought Bobby Moore to Craven Cottage in March 1974. Stock and Moore guided Fulham to the Cup Final. "Thank you for taking an old man back to Wembley" Bobby Moore enjoyed his time with Fulham from his goal against Crystal Palace to his 149th appearance, against Leyton Orient: Fulham 6 Orient 1.

Bobby Moore had friends and pupils (John Lacy) on the pitch plus many friends and pupils off the pitch. I remember a Friday evening out with friends and pupils in SW6 when we met Moore, Best and Marsh in an eel and pie shop. We were a little surprised to see such great men out and about on the eve of an FA Cup match. Marsh assured us that he would score the first goal. (He did.) Best rolled up his trousers to reveal the purple bruises from the battle of Stamford Bridge. (Thank you, Micky Droy.) Moore sat in the far corner and nodded off. Dreaming of Wembley 1966? Dreaming of Wembley 1975?

Gary Piper (our chaplain/youth coach/reserve goalkeeper) addressed the crowd before the match with Bournemouth on March 2nd 1993. Two minutes of silence followed. We mourned the passing of a gentle genius who chose to play his last 150 games with Fulham. Bobby Moore honoured Fulham, and his England partner George Cohen has made sure that July '66 is not forgotten at Craven Cottage or Loftus Road.

In the dark days between 1993 and 1997 I used to spend time in J block. Easily done on winter evenings when Fulham were playing nothing, midweek Autowindscreenwiper fixtures. The old wooden seats in the old wooden stands were empty and open to visitors (past and present). One such less than enthralling evening I noticed that Frank Lampard and Billy Bonds were up in J block. Presumably they were scouting—another look at Duncan Jupp. I attempted to make them welcome and asked if they had seen Bobby Moore that evening. Bonds looked at Lampard and Lampard looked up to the heavens. They moved on pretty quickly after that. It was, in fact, a serious question because many wise followers of Fulham have recorded encounters

in J block. Quigley and Turner have the details but Merula and Moore, Stock and Trinder, Keetch and Colonel Shrimpton, Cyril Swain…they have all been part of the struggle for survival.

Survival in the league, survival of the Cottage, survival at the Cottage; their work is far from done.

Bobby Moore's 600th league match was with Fulham at Roker Park. How appropriate that Sunderland should be our opponents on 1st March 2003—Fulham 1 Sunderland 0. "At least it was a victory and at least we won." His words massively understated Wembley '66 and yet captured exactly and precisely what we saw at Loftus Road in March 2003. At least it was a victory and at least we won.

Louis Saha heads the goal that won the Sunderland match at Loftus Road in March 2003.

Twerton

Almost as agonising as Ashford was Bath v Fulham at Twerton Park in November 1989. Non league Bath seemed set for victory in the first round of the FA Cup but Gary Peters and Clive Walker restored some pride and forced a replay. We eventually scraped through 2–1 at Craven Cottage thanks to a rare goal from John Watson, perhaps the least striking striker to lead the Fulham line in all my years at the Hammersmith End.

We saw a lot of Twerton Park that year because Bristol Rovers were in exile there, hence the routine league fixture in May 1989 plus another in September 1989, but to make matters worse the first leg of the divisional play-off took us back to Bath.

Bath is well placed for fast trains, Roman baths, Georgian terraces and four-star hotels. One distinguished follower of the Fulham took the bridal suite at the Royal Crescent Hotel for his visit to Twerton Park. (He was required to remove his black and white scarf from the balcony.) "Always the bridesmaid, never the bride"…that is the story of Fulham and play-offs. May 1989 saw us defend well for 88 minutes but the final score was Rovers 1 Fulham 0. It had been a day of great heat and no little frustration—frustration followed by sticks and stones hurled down upon us from a mound just above and behind the visitors' end. Twerton stewards were not willing to remove the hooligans but a police dog handler did send his alsatian to investigate.

From Twerton to the Cottage and 0–0 at half-time. A decent crowd, the best of the season (10,188), began to hope but Peter Scott was sent off and Nigel Martyn saved Ivor's best efforts. As we fell away, Rovers took control…one, two, three, four goals. Fulhamish, very Fulhamish and all too much for our Ivor: "Losing the play-off match to Bristol Rovers was the worst moment of my football career, worse even than the Derby match.

Fulhamish to go off the road just as promotion seemed possible.

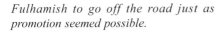

I took it very personally…I just burst into tears…that was the only time I haven't wanted to speak to supporters after a game."

That season we had four fixtures with Bristol Rovers: P4 W0 D1 L3; goals for: 0, goals against: 7. In six visits to Twerton Park we failed to score a goal and lost five of those six matches. The 0–0 in May 1989 was our best result. No wonder TOOFIF promised a statue in honour of the hero who scored the winner against Rovers—fast forward to Rob Scott in November 1997?

Twerton Park = "almost as agonising as Ashford" = litotes and meiosis and paradiastole. Twerton was worse than Ashford; much, much worse.

Underhill

May 1996: Barnet 3 Fulham 0—the grand finale to the worst season in our club's history. The season in which we flirted with relegation to the Conference and commanded 91st place in the league. Torquay away was terrible, Barnet away was humiliating. They let us off lightly in the second half when Sean Devine could have scored four or five goals. Every time they charged down that slope we fell over or simply waved them through. Micky Adams allowed some of the fringe players to prove their incompetence before moving them on.

Come February 1997 there was rather more steel about the Adams family—and there needed to be because Barnet, with not a little help from Mr Uriah Rennie, were in the lead twice. Conroy and Scott balanced the books and we departed for the Northern Line (27 stops via King's Cross) to Hammersmith. Normally I am a mild mannered old codger, especially after a precious point from a 2–2 draw, but not that Saturday. The sloping pitch, the slopping loos, the overzealous stewarding of a deserted stadium, the blatant injustice of the Barnet penalty, "Underhill, Underhill; awful, awful Underhill"—it all exploded on the march to the metro. Two distinguished Cambridge graduates and fellow followers of the Fulham (Emma Hawkey and Tim Taylor), plus Emma's mother, were witnesses to an outburst. An outburst and outrage followed by a solemn vow never, never to return to Underhill.

And, in one sense, that was that—but for the implications and complications of that visit to Barnet. Readers of *Following the Fulham*—

Survival and Celebration may cut out here, but others may not be aware of the importance of Underhill in the fight for Fulham and our search for saviours.

Immediately after the Barnet fixture I flew off to Borneo with the Muddyman plans for Craven Cottage plus letters to the Sultan of Brunei and his football coaches Kevin Keegan/Peter Beardsley/Paul Bracewell/Jim Pearson/Peter Osgood. From the ridiculous Underhill to the sublime Jerudong Park, from the poverty of Barnet FC to the infinite riches of the Sultanate. Several of my former pupils were involved with the Brunei Bullets (a palace XI which trained at the Royal Polo Club). The Bullets were a good side and getting better thanks to the quality of their coaches and guest stars. I was there to referee practice matches and to MC the main event. The occasion was also seen as an opportunity to present the FFC plans to the royal household, assisted by Kevin Keegan. The Muddymans had assured me that Ian Branfoot was working on KK while I was to court the Sultan's nephews.

All this had been discussed in the backroom of a pub near Underhill on the morning of the Barnet fixture. The Muddymans, the Shrimptons and I hoped to find the white knight among the golden domes of Jerudong. On my return to SW6 for Fulham 4 Scarborough 0 there was another plan and other planners. While the Sultan's team pondered proposals from Everton, Newcastle, Chelsea and Fulham the Harrods landau swept into the Cottage. The Brunei Bullets continue to take a kindly interest in Fulham. (Kevin Keegan always made sure that the welcome mat was properly prepared for their visits to the Cottage.) They come and go incognito and they have not been to Loftus Road. From Queen Victoria to his Royal Highness Prince Bahar, Fulham has welcomed monarchs and has provided palaces and parks for bishops. Royalty and the episcopate at Loftus Road or Underhill? Methinks not. Loftus Road and Underhill? We are NOT amused.

Fulham joy following Mike Conroy's goal at Underhill in February 1967.

Grounds We Love

Bournemouth, Blackpool, Brighton, Cambridge, Chester, Exeter, Grimsby, Hereford, Lincoln, Norwich, Oxford, Plymouth, Peterborough, Portsmouth, Scarborough, Shrewsbury, Southend, Swansea, Torquay, Wigan, Wrexham, York… Grounds we love because of location, location, location.

We love Chester. Ivor loved Chester. The only goal of the match in October 1980.

Grounds with cathedrals, and there are nine on the list above but to date only one (Lincoln) with the captain of FFC meditating before the match— Les Strong, that devout and cultured pilgrim from September 1981.

Grounds with ancient universities have special appeal; both Oxford and Cambridge were part of my education in the long ago and they both became part of Fulham's learning curve in the 70s. (1971–72 and 1974–75 we lost at Oxford; in 1979 we lost twice at Cambridge, the second defeat 4–0 in December 1979.) "FFC learning the hard way."

In fair weather both Oxford and Cambridge offer punting and picnics; in foul weather they have magnificent colleges/libraries/museums. Bristol and Nottingham have modern universities and ancient football clubs. Notts County (1862) and Nottingham Forest (1865) are founding fathers of the Football League. Bristol City (1897) and Bristol Rovers (1897) may not have quite the same status but they are both aristocrats compared with Oxford and

Happy memories of beach football.

Cambridge who only joined the league in recent times. Johnny Haynes was in his 11th season with Fulham when Accrington Stanley gave way to Oxford. Cambridge replaced Bradford Park Avenue in the Johnny Haynes era, just before his retirement in 1970. Follower of the Fulham and Oxford historian Nick Train treasured a shin pad worn by Haynes, while Cambridge lawyer David Roodyn had the Haynes, Keetch, Cohen triptych on his office walls. We had all made many, many trips to Nottingham and Bristol in the 60s (May 1969: Bristol City 6 Fulham 0) but Headington Manor and the Abbey Stadium were very new to us and added greatly to the pleasure of following the Fulham round the grounds.

Grounds we love beside the seaside, beside the sea and thus perfect for a great day out or even better a week-end away… Brighton, Exeter, Grimsby, Swansea, Split and Torquay feature elsewhere in these essays but we all have happy memories of beach football, fish and chips, sea and sand before the match. Indeed there were seasons such as 1993–94 when we had eight trips to the coast with much needed sea breezes to blow away the blues. The Premiership offers little to compare with Brighton's piers and the sands at Cleethorpes but there is comfort in Europe with Split offering sea, sun and a sensational stadium. Football to fireworks and a chance for Jean Tigana to win with Fulham where he had lost with Bordeaux.

The Valley

Charlton Athletic left The Valley in September 1985 and went into exile at Selhurst Park before moving on to Upton Park. Politics and economics confused and complicated the return to the Valley but Charlton Athletic did return and the stadium was reconstructed in a sensible and prudent manner.

Premiership status was achieved, again with good housekeeping. Our chairman may have talked of FFC as the "Man Utd of the south" but Fulham fans would prefer to be the "Charlton of the west" (provided that the same sensible and prudent housekeeping could achieve the reconstruction of Craven Cottage).

Congratulations to Charlton on the quiet revolution in their fortunes on and off the field. Not that it was always quiet at the Valley. In 1938 there were 75,000 spectators for a Cup game with Aston Villa. In 1946 Charlton reached the final of the FA Cup and in 1947 they beat Burnley to win the Cup. Sam Bartram was as famous at the Valley as Johnny Haynes was at the Cottage. Later Bartram lost out to Derek Hales in the Valley Review of Valiants. Hales first, Bartram second, Lee third.

I never saw Bartram but Hales, Peacock and Flanagan were very much part and parcel of the Ivor era. The promotion team of 1982 were unbeaten after six league games and we all set off for the Valley confident, over-confident, and lost 3–0. We struggled to a scrappy 2–1 victory at the Cottage in April. The next season saw the sad and somewhat mysterious departure of Malcolm Macdonald and an impressive piece of caretaking by Ray Harford. We went to the Valley in May and won a highly entertaining fixture 4–3. Paul Parker's own goal was as spectacular and uncalled for as Sava's in Berlin. Indeed comparisons between 1984 and 2003 are inevitable.

Then, as now, there was uncertainty about Craven Cottage. Then, as now, there was uncertainty about the managership of FFC. Then, as now, a trip to the Valley in May lifted the spirits. In the case of Ray Harford that victory at the Valley secured the hot seat; in 2003 the victory at the Valley did much to secure the hot seat for Coleman. In May 1984 Cliff Carr celebrated his goal by climbing into the South Stand; in May 2003 Luis Boa Morte celebrated victory by removing most of his clothes and hurling them to the Fulham fans. Capering about in his underpants Luis, Luis Bo was reliving his goal at Stamford Bridge. The Valley will never rival Chelsea Village but for followers of the Fulham the Charlton story is both inspiring and instructive.

End of term report, May 2003: All smiles on arrival in SE7, sunshine all the way down river from Putney Pier, an agreeable outing with GMB and BTCC, euphoria after the Everton own goals, safe for another season, and demob happy after ten months on tour with FFC.

All smiles at the final whistle: job done, match won, had fun…happy, clappy Valley. "Oh yes, most happy Valley, most happy Valley indeed!"

Vetch

In March 1982 Swansea beat Spurs to go top of the league. May 1986 Swansea back in the Fourth Division and February 2003 Swansea in 92nd place. Fulham were top of the Premiership for one week in August 2002 but they have been 91st. In May 1994, Swansea 2 Fulham 1 condemned us to the bargain basement; thus for some followers of the Fulham the Vetch Field is forever tinged with shame.

For others the Vetch has happier associations; the Mumbles shore, the university campus, the Dylan Thomas heritage trail combine to compensate for some indifferent football. Not that we have always floundered off the Mumbles; in 1983–84 we beat Swansea home and away with Ivor scoring twice at the Cottage and twice at the Vetch. In 1996–97 victory at the Vetch and a thriller at the Cottage confirmed our promotion credentials.

As poetic as Dylan Thomas: Mike Conroy scores at Swansea in September 1996.

My first visit to Swansea was a duty call—the Headmasters' Conference gathered there in 1987. When 300 headmasters get together on film (*Clockwise*) it is all good fun, but in reality one lot of top teachers teaching another lot of top teachers how to teach their teachers to teach, and all dragged out over three days, equals boring, boring, boring. I bunked off the evening session on the Tuesday to inspect the Vetch. Swansea were hosting/hostiling Cardiff. Police sirens blared and police dogs barked; there was a pitched battle at the railway station while up the road the Swans were hurling missiles at the Cardiff coaches. Fulham v Chelsea equates to a vicarage tea party in comparison with this "friendly" at the Vetch.

In October 1988 the Swansea fixture coincided with half-term so Sheila and I enjoyed a long week-end in Wales. It rained, of course, and Fulham lost, of course, but the spirit of the Dylan Thomas pub and the Dylan Thomas cottage and the Dylan Thomas boat house provided a comfort blanket. When the rain eased we could dig for lug worms on the Mumbles shore and recall scenes from *Under Milk Wood*.

Northampton and Swansea climbed the divisions in double quick time but hurtled back down just as swiftly. Fulham took 33 years to climb the greasy pole (1968–2001); can we hang on at the top or are we doomed to

Dylan Thomas with his wife and daughter Aeron.

lose our ground and our status? We do not want to do a Wimbledon nor do we wish to follow Northampton and Swansea. Let us take the advice of Dylan Thomas, let us "rage against the dying of the light."

My interest in Swansea dates from rugby football contacts in the 1950s; interest became affection as I followed the Fulham to the Vetch and affection warmed to devotion on learning that both Coleman and Melville were Swansea born. Swans to the rescue, Swans captaining us into the Premiership. Chris Coleman did more than lead us to the championship, he fought a greater fight, he raged against the dying of the light. What a triumph and how we cheered his return to health and mobility. And we cheered just as loudly when he was confirmed as our manager in May 2003.

Wembley

Bliss was it in that dawn to be alive,
but to be young (and Fulham?) was very heaven…

Fulham went to Wembley in May 1975, but (being Fulham) we took the scenic route. No other club has ever contested as many matches to get there—eleven—and few teams have insisted on doing it the hard way by failing to win the home leg in order to win away against opponents from a higher division. League leaders Everton were beaten at Goodison, Carlisle were overcome at Brunton Park, Birmingham were contained at Hillsborough and last gasped at Maine Road.

Following the Fulham to Wembley in '75 was an extraordinary experience because we were less than convincing in the second division and cannot have been any bookmaker's favourite for the fifth round, let alone a place in the final. Wise after the event, the experts stressed the experienced leadership of Mullery and Moore but those bookmakers would hardly have predicted two goals against Everton from Busby or two more from Mitchell against Birmingham. The sum of FFC proved greater than the parts and caused Mr Clough to pat the back of Alec Stock.

As for Tommy Trinder in his trilby, he loved it all. We, when we got round to believing it had actually happened, loved it too. Well, we loved getting to Wembley and we loved seeing OUR Fulham looking so elegant in their new suits. True they had forgotten to pack their shin-pads and the hero of the Carlisle match lost his form, but up until the kick-off it was just wonderful. After all those years and all those semi-finals we were there in the sunshine at Wembley. For many that was enough and for some of the team the first half was quite enough. Mervyn Day denied/defied us in that first half; Alan Taylor did for us twice in the second. Suddenly it was all over and we had lost but (being Fulham) we insisted on re-staging the event at Craven Cottage and won.

Great though it was to beat Bologna in the final of the Intertoto Cup and greater yet to be in Europe competing for UEFA honours, our one and only Wembley appearance has a special place in the hearts of the not so young followers of Fulham. Yes, grown men wept at the final whistle at Maine Road; the impossible had happened and we were off to Wembley.

Fulham's finest hour? Perhaps not, but, for most of us, Fulham's finest half hour.

Wimbledon

Bobby Grice followed the Fulham in the 60s until his doctor warned him that annual struggles to avoid relegation were bad for his blood pressure. Bobby was advised to follow a less stressful team—he opted for Wimbledon. The Dons may have been a sleepy old outfit in the 60s but by the time Bobby took the Thomsons to Plough Lane they inclined to craziness. Crazy enough to beat Burnley at Turf Moor and hold Leeds to a goalless draw at Elland Road. Crazy enough to charge from non-league to first division in ten years. Crazy enough to retain a place in the first division/Premiership for 12 years. Crazy enough to beat Liverpool in the final of the FA Cup in 1998.

All that success was too much for Bobby's heart and he died on the way to Wembley. Sheila and I rejoiced for him and for the Dons as they defied gravity and logic for so many years.

Plough Lane was a funny old ground with the away terraces stuck on top of a slag heap. The VIP area of the main stand was humble but homely and the Dons served a good strong cup of tea. I remember their cheerful acceptance of defeat in September '81. We beat them 3–1 but they seemed happy enough to be part of the third division. We were very fortunate to win 4–1 at the Cottage assisted by a timely OG. Fulham went up and the Dons returned to the fourth division—but not for long. In '85–'86 Wimbledon were far too strong for Fulham and brushed us aside as they were promoted and we were relegated. Onwards and upwards Wimbledon FC; 33 years in the wilderness for Fulham.

Salt in our wounds: promising young players Elkins and Jupp are sold on to Wimbledon. Coming the other way veteran striker Alan Cork. Looking more like Humpty Dumpty than lithe and lethal leader of the line (32 goals in '83–'84) Porky Corky huffed and puffed around the park but still scored two spectacular goals up at Scunthorpe before joining Micky Adams as coach/assistant manager. "Corky only has two moods: sullen, and depressingly sullen" (Simon Morgan—*On Song for Promotion*).

Come '99 Wimbledon returned to the Cottage for a cup tie and despite all their Premiership experience were beaten and well beaten by Bracewell's Fulham. Come November 2000 Tigana's Fulham were off to Selhurst Park to play the Dons. Wet and windy the day, muddy and bumpy the pitch but Louis Saha waltzed through twice and Hayles robbed Jon Harley to score the third goal. Wimbledon 0 Fulham 3. "Unstoppable, and three goals flattered Wimbledon" (Chris Coleman).

Fulham lost young fans to Wimbledon in the 1980s. As headmaster of Emanuel, I watched pupils drift away from Craven Cottage only to turn up in the playground with Crazy Gang regalia. I suspect that those fair-weather Dons will not be travelling to Milton Keynes. Will they be tempted to Loftus Road? Bobby Grice is with the spirits of J block—we need him and his generous smile.

Club 92

Club 92 membership is confined to those who have 'done' all 92 league grounds. Ken Ferris did them all in a single season 1994–95 (*Football Fanatic*, published by Two Heads, 1995). Other fans/fanatics take longer over their great trek. I started following the Fulham around the grounds back in 1951–52 and I have seen Fulham play at 92 different grounds but I haven't got the tie or the T-shirt because they are not 'The 92'. Cheltenham and Kidderminster for all their appeal have not yet appeared on the fixture list for Fulham and thus remain undone.

Turf Moor is very much of The 92 grounds but it has proved the undoing of many Fulham teams from April 1951 to February 2003. Burnley have proved uncivilized as well as invincible. Burnley managers, Burnley players but most especially Burnley supporters have been offensive/objectionable year in year out, worse even than Birmingham and Millwall. I refuse to go to Turf Moor even if it costs me a place in Club 92.

"The Stadium of Light is well worth a visit." All Arundel/Haverhill followers of Fulham told us so. Sheila and I set out for Sunderland on January 16th 2002. We flew to Edinburgh intending to take a train south on match day but we somehow ended up all at sea on the Royal Yacht. The wireless brought news of a precious point but we never saw Steed's goal and we may never add the Stadium of Light to the list of grounds achieved.

Hartlepool was on the agenda in 1994. What better way to see in the New Year? How appropriate to celebrate the chairman's OBE by following the Fulham to the North East. Plans were made but an SOS from another ground (Blagdons) took me south to assist an Old Emanuel XV. News of an away win (2–1) came via Fulham fan and master chef Pierre Carlier. Thus Hartlepool is another ground undone and now unlikely.

Never mind; I may not feature in the Club 92 handbook and I may never receive the Ken Ferris title of 'Football Fanatic' but my 92+ grounds have secured a higher honour. The Fulham programme notes for 23rd October 2002 contained the ultimate accolade. Our head of community, Captain Morgs, called me "that Fulham nut and genial eccentric". Thank you, Simon, for that and thank you, Simon, for so much else 1990–2003.

Jimmy Hill OBE and Roy Bentley, team-mates in the 60s, still going strong on and off the golf course.

Wanderers We

Merula wrote about "fair weather Fulhamites" back in 1907. They turned up at Christmas for the visit of Glasgow Rangers and only reappeared in March for the FA Cup tie with Manchester United. Merula contrasted such Fulhamites with those who journeyed around the grounds—to Anfield, of course, for the semi-final of the FA Cup (Fulham 0 Newcastle 6) but also to Gainsborough and Glossop, Clapton Orient and Leicester Fosse. *"About 500 of our supporters ventured up to Leicester—the 'bonny boys' and those 'poor wandering ones'— but, rest assured, they did not regret their journey."* (*The Cottagers Journals* for December 1907.)

Fast forward 77 years and there are still fans of FFC who support the team through thick and thin both home and away. Not just at Wembley in 1975 but in those relegation years when, as Simon Morgan admitted, the team were "****". They have known the dark days as well as more recent promotions and championships. This very season we met up with the "Ultra" of Athens, the "Torcida" of Split and the "Kilted" of Berlin—the mad, the bad and the dangerous to know. (Worse even than Birmingham, Cardiff, Leeds and Millwall.) With that fortitude required of all those who follow the Fulham we survived.

The Intertoto essays from August 2002 in the booklet *Following the Fulham into Europe* were dedicated to such fellow travellers. The dedication then was general, but below names are named in an attempt to add some local colour to this black and white snapshot, this Fulham photo.

Björn is front centre; Karen stands in front of her husband, Alan; Steve is in the cap, and Andy is in the goal; Brian in jacket; Derek in shirt; far right is Roger.

Björn: Hamburg based follower of the Fulham;

Andy and Brian: pioneer aviators—flew up to Newcastle for the promotion clash with Carlisle in April 1997;

Derek: the herald of Haverhill and timelord to the tour 1968–2003;

Arundel Roger: Captained us from the depths of the Torquay car park in 1996 to the heights of Blackburn and Huddersfield in April 2001;

Alan: sommelier from Bungay to Bologna and from Southwold to Sochaux;

Stephen: our expert on railways and pyrotechnics. Top train—the old Mark I; top bomb—Split.

"Mere man again succumbs to woman." Merula awarded prizes to Mrs Maude of Putney Bridge Road for her match reports from Hull and Derby in September 1907. In his editorial comments Merula seemed surprised that Mrs Maude had attended so many away fixtures. No such surprise these days. For the last 35 years Fulham's away support has been organised by Sandra Coles and Mary Doughty, with FSC and Fulham 2000 just as dependent on "woman"—Eva, Chris, Maureen, Samantha.

On our little corner of the Hammersmith End in the 1970s there were as many women as men *and* they followed the Fulham around the grounds:

Ollwyn, Sally, Janet and Di: the original golden girls—"All the way to Wembley";

Barbara and Elaine: "flutter, flutter"—fundraising for Fulham home and away;

Frances and Jan: stalwart supporters throughout the darkest days.

Karen: Eurostar and shrewd analyst—"More flair than flares in Zagreb";

Sheila: guide, philosopher and friend since 1980.

Thus wanderers, nomads, travellers, troubadours, vagantes…we have followed the Fulham over land and sea. In 1975 the FA Cup took us to Hull, Nottingham, Everton, Carlisle, Sheffield, Manchester and Wembley—over long and overdue. In 2002 Intertoto and UEFA cups took us into Europe, again over long and again overdue. Out of pocket perhaps, but this 'wandering one' prospered in Bologna, Split and Zagreb. The football and the fellowship are beyond price and probably beyond words.

Henceforth less of the 'poor wandering one' and more, much more, of the 'rich wandering we'.

Below: Mick and Ollwyn at Loftus Road, August 2003—
Fulham fans 1974 to 2003. Right: Elaine at the Valley,
May 2003.

Wolves

September 1959: Wolves 9 Fulham 0—the worst of many defeats at the old Molineux. In September 1997 there was a chance to inspect the new stadium, and the Riversiders organised a special coach from the Cottage for an evening game. The coach was luxurious, the tour of the ground was informative and the stewards took a real pride in the refurbished Molineux with its hall of fame. Place of honour in this hall of fame and in the match magazine went to William Ambrose Wright. Billy Wright = Wolves, just as Haynes = Fulham. With Wright the Wolves won everything; with Haynes the Fulham won promotion to the first division in 1958–59 but nothing much in the way of titles, medals or major trophies.

Fulham lost the match 1–0. Modest when compared with the nine goals in September '59 or the five in '76 or the five in '89. (Although we lost 5–2 that thrashing was somehow transformed/lifted/absolved by Ivor's record-breaking 158th goal.) In October 2000 the result was also transformed from a draw and a precious point into some sort of defeat when reinvented by the press: "You would think Wolves had won the FA Cup"—Rufus Brevett. After 11 wins this 0–0 was interpreted as vulnerability but not for long; Fulham ended the season as champions, ten places above Wolves for the first time since April '85.

For followers of the Fulham, the match of matches at Molineux was a second division fixture between Wolves and Super Mac's Fulham. Come 20th November 1982 we were third in the table and Wolves were fourth. Andy Gray was far too fast for Fulham in the opening minutes. Wolves went 2–0 ahead and seemed set for many more but just before half-time Ray Lewington scored with a thunderous volley. In the second half Ivor destroyed Joe Gallagher and suddenly we were in control. Final score 4–2 to Fulham and second place in the division. Having beaten Middlesbrough 4–1 away, Newcastle 4–1 away, Grimsby 4–0 away and now Wolves 4–2 away there was a real buzz about the team plus high, high hopes among the travelling supporters that we were heading for a second successive promotion.

Come Turf Moor and Boundary Park in March the legs and lungs had gone. Molineux was but a distant memory as followers of the Fulham returned defeated and dejected from Cambridge in April and Derby in May.

Sir Jack Hayward transformed Molineux into a magnificent modern stadium but the Wolves of the 90s have underperformed, underachieved and undermined the confidence of their chairman and fans. As for Fulham in '83 so for Wolves in 2002. Well clear of the pack with promotion in sight in March. Collapse in April, fourth in May. All very Fulhamish from the Wolves.

Fulham may not have matched the Billy Wright Stand, Fulham may never emulate Molineux, but at least (and at last) we do have two titles and an Intertoto Cup to set before Johnny Haynes.

York

Let the train take the strain and take the Topley tour to Bootham Crescent. One hour 58 minutes from King's Cross to York and a gentle stroll to the Minster before lunch at the Pavilion. The Pavilion has views of Fulford field where the good folk of York were slaughtered by Harald Hardrada. The survivors looked to London for help in 1066 and they looked to London again in 2002 when the Minstermen were on the brink of bankruptcy. Chairman Al Fayed donated £50,000 to the Save York City appeal. Terry Dolan, as manager of York City, was grateful but added "I don't think they'll be so generous on the pitch tomorrow." Come the morrow Fulham were generous enough in the first ten minutes allowing York space and time to have a go. Van der Sar was equal to their opening shots. Once Louis Saha had put Malbranque through Steed scored with ease and followers of the Fulham began to relax. Marlet killed the game off with a strong run and stronger finish. We could and should have scored more goals but the job was done. I had enjoyed my day out at an old fashioned ground in an old fashioned city. To be honest I enjoyed this cup tie much more than most of my visits to the great and famous Premiership grounds.

Enjoyment of Bootham Crescent has nothing to do with cramped seating, restricted views, antique loos and a heavy, lumpy, bumpy pitch. Enjoyment of the York City tie depends in no small part on enjoyment of the city itself—the magnificent minster, the ancient city walls, the quaint crescent which is Bootham and the chance to mingle with many old friends on the terraces. Highbury, Stamford Bridge, Villa Park are impressive enough and Pride Park is superb but you only see your immediate colleagues, those with whom you booked seats, with whom you travel and with whom you sit. It is almost impossible to catch up with Mark from the FA Cup run of '75, Charles the

Ivor fan from the 80s, Richard from *Cottage Pie* in the 90s, Chesterfield Pete and Rotherham Ray, etc, etc. At grounds such as Bootham Crescent it is easy to wander about before, during and after the game; such walking and talking is impossible in the Premiership.

York City avoided relegation but their finances remained/remain parlous. Fulham fans from 1987–1997 know that situation: living on the edge, living from week to week, living from hand out to hand out. "Fulham 2000" = "Save City 2002". We survived and York City are surviving (just surviving). It is this community of the terraces which made Bootham Crescent my ground of the season in 2001–2002. After 33 years in the wilderness Fulham were back with the Arsenals/Man Uniteds/Liverpools but I was not a happy chappy. My head said this is what Fulham needs and this is what followers of Fulham deserve but my heart was less sure.

Writing in 2003 when every Fulham fixture is away from Craven Cottage that day at Bootham Crescent grows in importance. York City 2002 should by now be somewhere down memory lane with Carlisle '75 and Carlisle '97 or safely lodged alongside those golden Goldstones of long ago, and yet, and yet, and yet it won't become a faded Fulham photo. It is more like the

stained glass window from York Minster: purgatory as depicted in 1153—colourful and painful. For Fulhamites and Minstermen in 2003 the picture remains just that: purgatorial. In purgatory are tortured and tormented souls. The Minstermen suffer but cling to their ancient home. Outwardly Fulham fans seem to prosper but inwardly we agonise so near and yet so far from the promised land. May 2003—further and further from the promised land.

Anxious and apprehensive the faces— York Minster 1153–2003 and Craven Cottage 1951–2003.

Grounds and Groundlings

Och aye, Don Mackay; ooh, aah Tigana. "O! It offends me to the soul to hear a rumbustious fellow split the ears of the groundlings." Shakespeare's Hamlet knew well the sufferings of spectators, mere groundlings who suffer for the team.

The groundlings of Fulham have suffered more than most over the years and this very week (27th March 2003) we have been mightily mocked: "no ground, no manager, no hope", and that was not at an away game, that was down by the riverside watching Head of the River races with friends and neighbours. House guests rejoicing in the departure of Tigana, Damiano and Propos. It offended me to hear rumbustious fellows split the ears with such jibes and taunts. All the better for Sheila's food, all the worse for my wine, these four Chelsea supporters mixed petulance with condescension. Petulant and self-pitying after defeats at home to Blackburn and Arsenal: "Same old Gunners, always cheating." Condescension and mockery at every mention of Fulham: "Pity about the Cottage, come to the Bridge; bring your Micky Mouse cup, put it alongside some real cups in our trophy cabinet." Years ago I might have asked to see their Tel Aviv tankard or talked about Good Friday 1977, but after 1987–1996 survival is enough for this groundling.

The Tigana years transformed our football and we were off to a flying start—P11, W11—and in the season of seasons we took the first division

La révolution franglaise

Avec des moyens colossaux, ses Français et une méthode efficace, Jean Tigana poursuit sa mission : faire de Fulham FC, qui rencontre Arsenal, ce samedi, puis Liverpool, un grand de la Premier League

Tributes to Tigana from the French press (L'Équipe, February 2003).

title with 101 points. At first the press were fulsome in their praise for our elegant football and Saha's 32 goals. Saha stormed Old Trafford with two more goals and we won our first Premiership match at the Cottage—Fulham 2 Sunderland 0—but by the time we had lost the semi-final of the FA Cup the honeymoon with the media was well and truly over.

Reporters demand attention and Tigana ignored them. At first they accepted the fiction that the manager's English was not up to press conferences, and they settled for John Collins and crumbs from the rich man's table. Later, however, they sensed that Tigana did not speak with them because he had no time for them. They became very critical of his inflexibility on and off the field. From the ranting Mike Parry on *Talk Sport* to the sophisticated Jon Henderson of *The Observer* the predictions came thick and fast throughout August 2002. "Tigana hot favourite in sack race." "Do it my way Tigana is still in charge but not for much longer." "Troubled Fulham, homeless and hopeless."

Scorn without, anxiety within plus exile at Loftus Road—a recipe for disaster; and yet, and yet, and yet…we beat Bolton 4–1 to go top of the Premiership. We beat Bologna 5–2 to win the Intertoto Cup. We drew with Manchester United and we beat Liverpool. Saha returned from injury to see off West Brom and Sunderland.

Fulham fans may not like Loftus Road but they still lift the loft with their "Ooh, aah, Tigana!" Most of us assumed that Tigana, Damiano and Propos would leave at the end of this season but I have yet to meet a single follower of the Fulham who questions what the three musketeers achieved in 2001. After Bracewell and 'brace yourself for stagnation' came the wind of change (le mistral?), a new leaner, fitter, faster Fulham. Old friends transformed—Hayles and Brevett much more confident; new friends acquired—Collins, Saha, Boa Morte, Goma. Not Premiership players according to Turnip Taylor, not as talented as Blackburn according to Sourness Souness but to us in the season of seasons they were majestic. Enchanted then, we may be older, wiser, wearier and warier now but we remain grateful to the magician Tigana, Merlin of Monaco.

Of all the Fulham managers between 1951 and 2003, the four remembered with the most affection are Stock, Macdonald, Adams and Tigana. Alec Stock took us all the way to Wembley and he always had time for a gracious word with Fulham fans. I remember in particular a long conversation at Dean Court when his health was poor and breathing difficult but he wanted to recall old friends from Craven Cottage.

My French is adequate, the lawyer's French is good, Muriel and Piers speak perfect French but Tigana is not interested in small talk. A discussion document presented in French (checked by the lawyer, double checked by Piers) was received with a smile but remains without comment. Macdonald and Keegan were prompt in providing detailed answers to specific questions.

Andre Maurois wrote about a distinguished leader (Colonel B) who was both enigmatic and silent. Colonel B observed, Colonel B reflected, Colonel B did not court affection, Colonel B was a man of few words, Colonel B was a man of action. *Les silences du Colonel Bramble* 1917. Jean Tigana did not court affection, was a man of few words, a man of action. Le silence du Colonel Tigana. February 2000 to April 2003. Alec Stock, Super Mac and Micky Adams may have been closer to the fans but Tigana achieved a championship, Premiership survival and European football. Formidable for Fulham or, as they say in French, "*formidable!*"

Zagreb

Back to Croatia for another round of the UEFA Cup. After the magnificent facilities at Split the Maksimir Stadium was gaunt and battle scarred. The 1990 riot on the pitch with Serb police using batons to discipline Dinamo players relaunched the Balkan Wars. The stadium tour included an examination of recent bullet holes. Veterans of the Intertoto were used to armed police and troops with riot shields. Barked at frequently but thus far not shot at we were apprehensive on arrival in drizzle, apprehensive as there was no cover, apprehensive given the extreme hostility of the Croatians in Split.

The drizzle eased just before 5pm—an early evening game but no lack of support for Dinamo Zagreb. From the far end of the stadium came a mighty roar of DEEEEEENAMOW and from the flanks came back the yet mightier

Matchday in Zagreb. We gather quietly at the Palace Hotel, they gather loudly at Zagreb Station.

response ZAAAAAAARRRRRRRRRGREB. In 52 years at 90-plus grounds I have never heard such a sound. Goodness knows what Dinamo v Split must be like, much noisier than Fulham v Chelsea and much more daunting than the Pompey chimes or the Millwall moan or the Roker roar.

On the team sheets the most significant name is that of Senor Gonzales. We had admired Spanish officials on the Intertoto circuit and on 31st October 2002 the first Dinamo lunge at Luis Boa Morte brought a red card. Never mind the where of the tackle (well away from goal), never mind the when of the tackle (early in the game), Polovanec was 'Off' and from then on Boa Morte tormented the Croatians. He scored the first goal which forced Dinamo to answer the passionate supplications of their fans for rather more attacking football. We soaked up the pressure and then Marlet killed the game with the second goal. Stolcers set up Hayles who iced the cake.

David Shrimpton and his sons (third and fourth generation Fulham) phoned home with the good news from the terraces while Bill Muddyman waved to us from the VIP box. 31st October is Halloween is trick and treat with (for once) Fulham mastering the tricks and the travelling fans enjoying the treat. Our 200 could not match their 30,000 for noise but we could sing and we could dance.

November 1st is All Saints Day, a major festival in Zagreb. If there were 30,000 at the Maksimir Stadium for the Fulham game there were 90,000 at the Mirogoj Cemetery. Sheila and I were at the cathedral as bus after bus transported pilgrims to the family tombs. All morning, all afternoon, all evening the families of Zagreb took flowers and lanterns to the shrines at Mirogoj. On the Thursday evening at 5 o'clock Senor Gonzales officiated at the Dinamo fixture. On the Friday evening at 5 o'clock the Archbishop of Zagreb officiated at the Festival of Lights.

31st October 2002. 5pm, the match; 8pm, the celebrations.

Both events illustrated Croatian faith in action, both events proved that Zagreb is more civilized than Split. The head porter at the Hotel Esplanade explained the difference between Dinamo fans and the Torcida of Hajduk Split. "Many times I have been in Split; believe me they are mad, believe me they are bad, believe me they are dangerous to know."

This away win in Zagreb must rank with Goodison Park in February '75 (Everton 1 Fulham 2), with Super Mac's side winning 4–1 at Newcastle in October '82 and with seeing off the sourness of Souness at Ewood Park in April 2001—Blackburn 1 Fulham 2. The European tour has given us three great away days: Bologna, Split, Zagreb—these three, but the greatest of these is Zagreb.

Following the Fulham Around the Grounds. This A to Z began in the modest surroundings of Ashford and Barnet, but at last and at least, comes Z for Zagreb and Fulham are in Europe. Gone is the gallows humour of 1996 and just for a moment it IS all over, the fat lady IS singing, and the song she is singing is, of course, a song for Europe: "Viva El Fulham".

Merula may or may not have been a fat lady but he too could sing: "In the moment of victory one is apt to ascribe more flattering laudations than the occasion merits but penning these notes some days after the event I am still of the opinion that our bonny boys did right gloriously." As for Merula in March 1908 so too this very autumn in Bologna, in Split and in Zagreb "our bonny boys did right gloriously."

Farewell to Finlay Street

In 1946 the Thomsons left Scotland for London SW. We lived in a flat at Exeter House, thus summers meant cricket on Putney Heath and winters meant football in Bishop's Park. Finlay Street in 1947 was just a happy accident, a convenient short cut from the bus stop to the park. In 1951 the

"On the bench." Young fans from 1951 with the author in the centre and his sister Judi at far right.

footballers of Finlay Street matured into followers of the Fulham and the rest is *Survival and Celebration*. Rituals were developed with Finlay Street becoming Pilgrims' Way in the 60s and 70s. Meet at the junction of Finlay Street and Stevenage Road, buy programmes and head for the Enclosure, gossip outside the Black and White shop while awaiting latecomers. Enter the Hammersmith End at 2.30 sharp, meet up with Mick, Ollwyn (and her three daughters), little Mark, Philip, Mr and Mrs B. Of the Finlay Street four, Peter Kitchen (like his namesake, the expensive striker) was only with us for a couple of seasons. Bill lasted until he took to golf. Roy is still in business in Fulham and advertises from time to time in the programme but I haven't seen him at a match since the Cup Final. PFT, Peter K, Bill and Roy are the Finlay Street four from 1951.

Of those Exeter House children and Finlay Street footballers just two remain devoted to FFC, one as a season ticket holder, the other following from afar (Vancouver BC) but present in person for our first UEFA Cup victory over Hajduk Split. My sister (far right in the picture) has put up with me and with Fulham for 53 years and has been extraordinarily patient, smiling when I met her plane at Heathrow and then abandoned her at Hammersmith in order to catch the second half of Fulham 4 Burnley 0 in December 1998.

Finlay Street as Via Dolorosa. With heavy hearts Sheila and I paused on the corner of Finlay Street to purchase programmes for the Egaleo match in

July 2002. The last programme for the final fixture at Craven Cottage proper, which is not to say that a new Craven Cottage would be improper, simply that it would not and could not be quite the same.

With a heavier heart I returned to Finlay Street in April 2003 to take photographs and (with permission from Motspur Park) to revisit J Block and the boiler rooms. Revisiting and reliving hundreds of matches; revisiting and reliving dozens of conversations with Steve Magee.

Farewell then Finlay Street—another season at Loftus Road and then? In 1947 when I first visited Finlay Street half the residents were followers of the Fulham. As late as the Cup Final the bunting was out as the street parties honoured FFC. Come the championship years of 1999 and 2001 the affluent folk of Finlay Street were funding the campaign to stop our new stadium. Chairman frustrated, fans infuriated, stadium on hold or sold—who knows? Fulham friendships and Fulham memories, however, remain inviolate, sacrosanct and sublime. Look at page 143 of Ken Coton's *Fulham Photos*— the birds are singing in Bishop's Park and some of their songs still echo around Craven Cottage and Finlay Street.

Birdsongs of Finlay Street

1907, singing in Finlay Street: Merula being translated "blackbird"; Merula has a rich repertoire of songs, melodic, mellow, fluting with a distant desolate tone.

1951–2002, singing in Finlay Street: Melanitta being translated "common Scot"; this common Scot has a limited repertoire—loud piping, regularly repeated.

1896–2003, and still singing at the Cottage End of Finlay Street: Alcidae being translated "auks" aka "the black and whites". These black and whites offer their noisy repertoire of chattering notes, turning to a laughing, buzzing chorus. See Mullarney and Grant *Complete Field Guide to Birds of Britain*, Harper Collins.

And the answer is: August 2004!

Hold the Back Page

All those years following the Fulham around the grounds and not a word in this book of White Hart Lane… Why no talk of Tottenham?

What about April 1948 (Tottenham 0 Fulham 2)? Over the hills and far away—the Malvern Hills where I attended a very strict boarding school without so much as access to a wireless set. Thereafter it was just one near miss after another each time I went to White Hart Lane.

Near miss with my son Ian on his 10th birthday treat, 10th September 1977. Good goal from John Mitchell but it was disallowed and we lost 1–0. *Match of the Day* cameras suggested that it was indeed a good goal, a very good goal, but the result remains Tottenham 1 Fulham 0.

Near miss when Sheila and I were at White Hart Lane for the fourth round of the League Cup in December 1981. Fulham from the third division stretched the mighty Spurs with Dean Coney outstanding but we lost 1–0.

Near miss in the FA Cup in January 1984. 0–0 at the Cottage and a roughing-up at White Hart Lane. Roberts and Co were roundly condemned by the press but Spurs knocked us off the ball and out the Cup 2–0.

And so on and so on. Thus, despite some terrific victories over Spurs at the Cottage and Loftus Road, there was little to lure me back to Tottenham this season. Even less incentive after the Everton result but, cometh the 30th August 2003, cometh the lawyer with the lunch, the limo and two tickets on the halfway line, far from the Fulham fans.

2.45pm - Tottering among the Tottenham (apprehensive and anxious as always) with confident cockerels crowing all around us.

3.00pm - Sitting in silence surrounded by 33,000 noisy Tottenham supporters. All the team and most of the fans wearing THOMSON shirts—could this be Split all over again? Certainly there were Spurs as strident as Croats with all the old taunts: "There for the taking, Fulham's there for the taking"; "Down with the Boro. You're going down with the Boro!"

3.23pm - Sitting in silence surrounded by 33,000 disbelieving Tottenham fans. Fulham 1 Spurs 0 after a sensational solo goal from Barry Hayles.

3.45pm - Half time and a walk to the visitors' end. All smiles over there.

4.23pm - Sitting in silence surrounded by 32,500 irate Spurs as Anderton and Richards gifted the second goal to Hayles.

4.27pm - Sitting in silence surrounded by 31,000 shell-shocked Spurs as Hayles set up Boa Morte for the third goal.

4.30pm - David and I have elbow room, leg room and the pick of five thousand seats. "All gone quiet over here, all gone home over here."

5.10pm - Seven Sisters Road—singing and dancing as David and I meet up with fellow followers of the Fulham astounded at the ease and elegance of the victory.

Chauffeur driven to the Hammersmith line by David in good time to call my publisher: "Hold the back page…! Thank you, David; thank you, Fulham.

Cold light of dawn and the questions: How good were we? How bad were Spurs? Brian Glanville's verdict: "Dismal Spurs pounded by Fulham." Dave Kidd on Hayles: "Has a massive heart and an eye for goal." *Talk Sport* (positive for once): "Fulham were excellent; all credit to Chris Coleman."

Early days and early doors but an away win was important. But an away win at White Hart Lane? Rare and precious indeed.